Interventions is produced on the land of the Wurundjeri people of the Kulin Nation. We acknowledge the Traditional Owners of country throughout Australia and recognise their continuing connection to land, waters and culture. We pay our respects to their Elders past, present and emerging. Their land was stolen, never ceded. It always was and always will be Aboriginal land.

THE NEIGHBOUR FROM HELL

Two Centuries of Australian Imperialism

Tom O'Lincoln

INTERVENTIONS
MELBOURNE

Dedication

This book is dedicated to Nancy Aitkin and Nic Maclellan, Tom's neighbours for many years in Albert Street, Brunswick. They shared many good times and a common commitment to political activism. When this book was first published, the joke was that they might be the neighbours referred to. On the contrary: when Tom became ill, they helped and supported him and provided a welcoming place for him to spend time.

First published 2014 by Interventions Publishers
2nd edition with new Introduction 2021 by Interventions Inc

Interventions is a not-for-profit, independent, radical book publisher. For further information:
  www.interventions.org.au
  info@interventions.org.au
  PO Box 24132
  Melbourne VIC 3001

Design and layout of this edition by Viktoria Ivanova.
Cover design from cartoon by "Hop" (Livingston Hopkins), "Annexation – carrying the blessings of civilisation into New Guinea", The Bulletin Vol. 1, no. 4, 9 June 1883, p. 13.

Author: Tom O'Lincoln

Title: The Neighbour From Hell: Two Centuries of Australian Imperialism
ISBN: 978-0-6452534-5-0: Paperback
ISBN: 978-0-6452534-4-3: eBook

© Tom O'Lincoln 2014

The moral rights of the author have been asserted.
All rights reserved. Except as permitted under the Australian Copyright Act 1968 (for example, a fair dealing for the purposes of study, research, criticism or review), no part of this book may be reproduced, stored in a retrieval system, communicated or transmitted in any form or by any means without prior written permission.

All inquiries should be made to the publisher.

A catalogue record for this work is available from the National Library of Australia

Contents

Preface	1
Author's introduction 2014	3
Introduction to the second edition	7
Robbers & spoilers	17
Two world wars and neo-colonialism	41
Riders on the storm	49
Testing the Vietnam Syndrome	73
Further reading	91
Endnotes	93
Tom O'Lincoln Legacy Project	105

Preface

The first edition of this book was published in 2014. In that the author noted that a version of the second chapter appeared as 'Australian Imperialism in the Cold War' in *Marxist Left Review* no. 6 2013 and that part of the final chapter appeared in the collection *Class and Struggle in Australia*, edited by Rick Kuhn (Pearson Education 2005). He remarked that the general line of argument arose from an insight which Dave Nadel drew to his attention, derived from Humphrey McQueen's *A New Britannia* (Penguin 1970). David Glanz and Phil Griffiths were early contributors to the development of the ideas contained in the book, and Nic Maclellan and Rick Kuhn also contributed substantially during the writing of the book. The first edition was supported by the Jeff Goldhar Project.

This second edition was undertaken because the first edition was out of print, and we considered it important to retain availability of this short introduction to the role of Australia's boutique imperialism. While there have been minor corrections and amendments to the text throughout and to the references, the text remains very close to the author's original work. This edition is enhanced by the inclusion of a new introduction by Sam Pietsch. Sam has brought the analysis up to date, primarily by reviewing the ongoing and rapid rise of China as an economic and political power. The seven years since the first edition have not seen any diminution in the significance of the central theses of this book; rather, the main arguments have been strengthened and their urgency heightened.

A number of people assisted with comments, production and other help in both editions.

In the first edition, Tom expressed his gratitude for comments, production and other help to: Jane Tovey, Janey Stone, Liz Ross, Rick Kuhn, Corey Oakley,

Les Thomas and Ben Hillier. For mistakes and weaknesses, Tom noted the responsibility was entirely his.

For this second edition thanks in addition to Sam Pietsch for the new introduction and for assistance with the text, Alex Ettling for helpful comments, to Eris Harrison for copy-editing and Vik Ivanova for the design and layout.

We are also very grateful to the following people whose financial assistance made this new edition possible: Graeme Haynes, Anne Lawson, Tess Lee-Ack, Dave Nadel, Liz Ross, Robert Stainsby, Fleur Taylor, Phillip Whitefield and Robert Zocchi.

This second edition is the first book in a project to publish new editions of all Tom O'Lincoln's major works, ensuring that they will be available in perpetuity through print-on-demand services. Interventions is proud to be able to make this contribution to supporting the continued availability of Tom's enduring contribution to socialist history and analysis.

Author's introduction 2014

'Another Australian expeditionary force' is a familiar phrase to the world. Australians have fought on more battlefronts than any other men since the time of Genghis Khan.

Washington Post correspondent Richard Oulahan[1]

The world is a complex, volatile place; yet, some things become familiar. When Australia fights an overseas war in, for example, Afghanistan alongside the US, responses on the broad left generally fit a pattern. Critics will point to Australia's dependence on the US. This is undeniable – most states in the world depend on US power in some way. From that recognition, however, the left generally proceeds to a much more questionable argument, lamenting what it sees as chronic Australian subservience towards the big-power ally. The US is accused of dragging this country into wars that are not in 'our' interest.

For example, Alison Broinowski's book *Howard's War* makes a telling critique of the 2003 invasion of Iraq. She complains that, 'instead of standing up for Australia... Howard bent over backwards to oblige Washington and London.' Regarding the government's passivity about the fate of Australians in Guantanamo, she asks: 'What makes us so meek?'[2] In much the same way, such astute historians as Ray Evans and Henry Reynolds see this country as fighting foreign wars at 'the behest of the British or American hegemon.'[3]

I can't agree. These views amount to a psychological interpretation without much structural or strategic content. More importantly, Australia isn't 'meek' at all. It's an imperialist power in its own right. It has sent troops to distant wars to gain credit with Britain and, more recently, the US, hoping that these 'great and powerful friends' will back up Australia's interests in our own region. This has been a pattern for well over a century. It doesn't make Canberra a 'lapdog' for the US. In 1962, journalist Dennis Warner described it more accurately as 'life insurance that we're taking out' to back up Australia's own interests.[4] It's part of a strategy for leveraging power, a sort of boutique imperialism in which Canberra manoeuvres carefully to maximise its clout. That is a key theme of this book.

According to analyst Jeff Doyle, 'Australia is an outrider of an English speaking Empire whose symbolic capital once was London and is now Washington.'[5] He needed to add that the 'outrider' also influences what happens at the core and that it promotes what it sees as its (bourgeois) national interest across the globe. The Australian Secret Intelligence Service (ASIS) even sent one of their number to Chile to help bring down the leftist Allende government.[6] It is important to be clear on the imperialist nature of the Australian state; otherwise, we misunderstand our enemies. Important though it is to fight the evils of US imperialism, this book argues that, in Karl Liebknecht's famous words, the main enemy is in our own country.[7]

A Marxist study of imperialism must touch on Lenin. My approach echoes Lenin's main themes.[8] He, along with Bukharin, saw the outbreak of a great imperialist war in 1914 as linked to an alignment of capital and the state. This was occurring within individual countries and on a global scale; it was associated with the exploitation of what today we call the Third World; and it had laid the basis for launching revolutionary struggles. Such horrors still feature in the world today. In the midst of the Western onslaught on Iraq and Afghanistan, the operation of something resembling Lenin's schema was surely undeniable. These were undoubtedly what he would call 'annexationist, predatory wars of plunder...wars for the division of the world.'[9] Just to make it more blatant, Americans got to see Bechtel Corp and Haliburton aligned with the US military via Vice President Dick Cheney.

On the other hand, critics have identified weaknesses in Lenin's argument. The export of capital to the Third World is not a dominating factor in the global imperialist system, as Lenin believed; and reformism in the Western labour movement can't be explained by a transfer of wealth from the colonies to a privileged section of the working class, as Lenin also thought.[10] Confusions of this kind are hardly surprising. Lenin was engaged in an urgent recasting of Marxist theory overall, with the aim of understanding the global catastrophe of the war and charting a path to socialist revolution. The ideas he got out of such an ambitious project, nearly a century ago, are bound to look a bit rough today.

The specifics of Australian history pose further challenges to constructing a Leninist analysis. If imperialism is identical with the 'monopoly stage of capitalism,' as Lenin argued, did colonial Australia fit the bill? If an imperial power is, ipso facto, 'ripe' for nationalisation – as Lenin believed – can that apply to antipodean colonial enterprises? The Colonial Sugar Refining Company (CSR) was an imperial company. Otherwise, I doubt it. There is also a concern with timeframes: Lenin thought that the 'highest stage of competition was 1860–70,'[11] but, in Australia, that period was also the launching pad for a specifically Australian empire. Far from providing a haven for laissez-faire, colonial governments launched a 'development strategy' building several types of transport infrastructure and urban utilities, communications systems, education facilities and agricultural research.[12] We can, of course, take refuge in the fact that, as Lenin obviously realised, there were earlier social forms bearing the name imperialism. That, however, raises as many problems as it solves.

To understand the peculiar role Australia has come to play in the imperial system, we also need to consider something Lenin understandably paid little attention to. For him, the 'whole world' was divided into a large number of oppressed nations and an 'insignificant number of oppressor nations, which command colossal wealth and powerful armed forces.'[13] So, which category does Australia fit? Neither seems adequate, and there are clearly intermediary types of states. Australia is obviously not an oppressed nation, even though its leaders are constrained by their weakness relative to the great powers; but neither does it possess colossal wealth and power. In its earlier decades, it came closer to resembling a third category: that of a frontier of imperialism driven by colonial settlers such as the South African Boers or the *Pied-Noirs* in North Africa. They spearheaded the looting of the local people in a particular version of what Karl Marx called the 'primitive accumulation of capital.'[14]

Aghiri Emmanuel described the peculiar dynamic of settler nationalism. For settlers, 'the colonial adventure was…the mainspring of their existence and their supreme justification. They benefited from colonialism and therefore promoted it, without reserve or contradiction.' This, ironically, could bring them into conflict with the mother country, which was less fanatical about imperial expansion in the settlers' neighbourhood because the rulers at home had a global perspective.[15] That didn't make them progressive. Such states were complicit in the imperial project, but they can't be boiled down to Lenin's definitions. The relevance of 19th century Australia should be evident. Since Federation, the Australian bourgeoisie has developed a more sophisticated and diversified role in the imperialist framework, including its own independent national state. The strategy underlying what's often called a capitalist 'insurance policy' remains as a red thread tying together two centuries of imperialist manoeuvres on this continent. But the relationship with Lenin is somewhat tangled; and, rather than rush what is shaping up as a long and complex literature review to untangle it, I have chosen to apply a fairly simple alternative methodology.

What is imperialism? It's this. The core objectives of an imperialist state are stability and security for profits and trade routes, with the aim of creating the best possible conditions for capital accumulation.[16] In 1994, British Foreign Secretary Lord Lansdowne expressed it in terms of the need to watch over, foster and protect imperial interests. This concern is reflected in Australians' reference to an 'arc of instability' in the islands to our north.[17] Of course, it can be said that even the smallest and weakest states try to achieve favourable conditions for business. The point is that the stronger states can impose them on the weak, giving rise to oppression and uneven development. That in turn leads to an asymmetrical culture of benefits, expectations and behaviour on the various sides. This book traces that contradictory process as it works its way through Australian history.

Introduction to the second edition

The Neighbour from Hell was first published in 2014. This new edition is testament to its ongoing relevance as a history of Australian foreign relations written from a political perspective of international solidarity and anti-imperialism, rather than from the usual nationalist outlook. This introduction will not attempt to update the original book to cover comprehensively events in the intervening years but will simply indicate how its themes can be applied today to the changing international context in which the Australian state operates.[18]

By far the most important development is the ongoing and rapid rise of China as an economic and political power. Between 1999 and 2019, China's economy grew by a staggering 460 per cent in real terms. As a proportion of the United States economy, China rocketed from just 17 per cent to 63 per cent over the same period.[19] The total size of the economy is not the only relevant measure of economic development, but it provides an overall indication of the scale of China's advance. Underwritten by this economic growth, Chinese military spending grew by nearly 580 per cent between 1999 and 2019. At the beginning of this period, the US outspent China by a factor of 10 to one on its military; in 20 years, the ratio had fallen to three to one.[20] So, although the US remains by far the stronger power, the gap is appreciably diminishing. This is particularly so in the Asia-Pacific region, where China can concentrate its resources, while the US has 'responsibilities' stretching around the globe.

It is this change in the relative balance of power which is fuelling confrontation between the two imperialist rivals, to a degree not seen since the end of the Cold War. The Chinese ruling elite is no longer prepared to accept a regional order based around the dominance of the US, established through its victories in World War II and the Cold War. Fearful of being encircled by US forces operating out of bases in Japan, South Korea and Australia, China has invested heavily in modernising its air force, navy and missile defences. The first two Chinese aircraft carriers, the prime asset of a modern naval power, were commissioned in 2012 and 2019. Tiny islands in the South China Sea have been fortified to back up expansive territorial claims. The aim is to at least challenge the US navy's ability to operate with impunity in the waters immediately bordering China.

It is a challenge that the US cannot simply ignore if it wishes to retain its pre-eminence in East Asia. Barack Obama's 'Pivot to Asia', announced in 2012, was never fully implemented, but it revealed an intention to refocus US resources on confronting China. The Trump presidency saw rising diplomatic tensions, culminating in the imposition of trade sanctions aimed at curbing Chinese manufacturing exports and preserving the US industrial base. This departure from liberal doctrines of free trade was not some aberration of Trumpian populism, but expressed the generally agreed opinion of US ruling circles that a tougher stance on China was required.

We have, then, entered a dangerous new phase of international relations in the Asia-Pacific, in which the US–China rivalry forms a filter through which all other developments must be viewed.

This inter-imperial competition is not foregrounded by O'Lincoln in the concluding chapter of *The Neighbour from Hell*, which deals with a period characterised by the domination of more peripheral states by the US and Australia, through warfare in Iraq and Afghanistan and through neo-colonialism in the South Pacific. Nonetheless, the general analytical framework employed by O'Lincoln retains its relevance. He identifies Australia as a 'boutique imperialist' nation, meaning that it is not among the first rank of global powers but nevertheless possesses a developed capitalist economy and substantial military power. The Australian state uses these resources to defend the specific interests of the Australian ruling class within the Asia-Pacific region. The alliance with the US is a strategy pursued to further these aims. It strengthens Australia's ability to fulfil its own imperialist ambitions, rather than demonstrating a lack of independence.

The rise of China as a major power represents the greatest challenge to Australian interests since the defeat of Japan in World War II. China's rapid economic growth underwrote the longest period of continuous economic growth in the history of Australian capitalism. By 2018–19, exports to China were valued at over $150 billion annually, amounting to nearly one-third of the total.[21] But a contradiction between Australia's ever increasing trade links with China and the close military and strategic partnership with the US is clear.[22] For a while, it seemed this contradiction could be contained. The *2013 Defence White Paper* argued optimistically that: 'The Government does not believe that Australia must choose between its longstanding Alliance with the United States and its expanding relationship with China; nor do the United States and China believe that we must make such a choice.'[23] Australia was even cast, somewhat hopefully, in the role of potential mediator between Beijing and Washington.

These hopes were short lived. The *2020 Defence Strategic Update* frankly noted that 'Strategic competition, primarily between the United States and China, will be the principal driver of strategic dynamics in our region.'[24] The response was Australia's own version of the 'Pivot to Asia', in the form of hundreds of billions of dollars of spending on advanced weapons systems, boosting capacity for military intervention anywhere in maritime Southeast Asia or the Pacific islands.

That Australia would ally with the US in its confrontation with China was never seriously in question. The latter's importance as an export market simply does not outweigh the benefits of Australia's close ties with the US, still the world's largest economy and strongest military power. Moreover, the geopolitical status quo in the Asia-Pacific has been of enormous benefit to Australian capitalism over the decades. The decline of relative US power, on the other hand, raises the spectre of a politically and geographically isolated Australia confronting a hostile China. As O'Lincoln charts, such fears have been a constant of Australian strategic thinking since the late 19th century. So Australia is eager, where possible, to reinforce the US commitment to the region and the alliance itself. Australia agreed, for example, to host a detachment of 2,500 US marines in Darwin from 2012, an ongoing reminder of Australia's usefulness as a southern anchor point for military operations in Asia.

10 THE NEIGHBOUR FROM HELL

Leaders in bright red, blue and yellow patterned shirts at the Pacific Island Forum, Tuvalu 2019. Australian Prime Minister Scott Morrison is fifth from right. Photo: Nic McLellan

Nonetheless, Australia continues to navigate the demands of alliance politics while defending specific interests which do not align with those of the US. More reliant economically on exports to Asian countries than is the US, Australia has so far remained more committed to free-trade doctrines. In 2020, Prime Minister Scott Morrison obliquely criticised Trump's policies, arguing that 'abrasive or confrontational trade relationships' could undermine political partnerships.[25] Australia and the US both reject Chinese territorial claims in the South China Sea, a vital route for commercial and military shipping. But Australia has so far rejected US requests to participate in so-called 'freedom of navigation' operations – in which military ships or aircraft deliberately violate these claims – judging them to be too provocative.[26] Such policy nuances continue the trend, identified by O'Lincoln, whereby Australia does not simply follow US dictates on every issue but attempts to actively shape the alliance relationship in its own favour. Exactly how much room for manoeuvre will remain as the China–US confrontation develops in coming years is an open question.

Another of O'Lincoln's major themes is ongoing neo-colonialism among the Pacific island nations. This is Australian imperialism's area of special concern, where even the US must take a back seat. But here, too, the intensifying rivalry with China has renewed the prospect of penetration by 'outside' powers. In 2016, Australia responded with the 'Pacific step-up' policy, aimed at maintaining its pre-eminence. To counter increasing Chinese naval activity, Australia provides Pacific nations with naval patrol boats and aerial surveillance capability, under the 'Pacific Maritime Security Program.'[27] In 2018, Australia concluded a deal to redevelop the Lombrum Naval Base on Manus Island, off the north coast of Papua New Guinea (PNG).[28] Originally constructed as a staging post in the offensive to drive Japan from Southeast Asia during World War II, the revitalised base will now help Australia and the US ward off China's challenge in the Indonesian archipelago and Southwest Pacific Ocean.

Although still dwarfed by military spending, Australian aid funding for the Pacific has been increased, supplemented by a loans scheme for constructing infrastructure. This is in response to China's 'Belt and Road' initiative, which offers Pacific nations an alternative source of finance. In 2018, Australia hurriedly stepped in to fund construction of a new undersea internet connection

INTRODUCTION TO THE SECOND EDITION   13

Australian Defence Force aid delivery. Photo: Department of Defence

between PNG, Australia and the Solomon Islands, which was going to be financed by China. This was seen as an unacceptable infringement on Australian interests, considering the economic importance and strategic sensitivity of modern communications infrastructure. An Australian company was subsequently awarded the contract for construction, freezing out Chinese communications giant Huawei.[29]

Although this sort of competition may seem a boon to the Pacific nations, it comes at a cost. The major powers assume that financial assistance will bring influence over local governments, all the more so in some of the world's least developed economies. Australian aid amounts to 8 per cent of the PNG Government's usual budget.[30] Australia provided an extra $440 million loan in 2019 to cover a budget shortfall, with China also reportedly prepared to offer assistance.[31] Financial dependence allows Australia to determine spending priorities, and Australian personnel are directly deployed in PNG's military, police force and public service.

Nor will competition between Australia and China do anything to address the most pressing challenge faced by Pacific island nations – climate change.

Scott Morrison (Australian Prime Minister) and Enele Sopoaga (Tuvalu Prime Minister) at Pacific Island Forum Tuvalu 2019. Photo: Nick McLellan

The joint communiqué issued by the Pacific Islands Forum in 2019, agreed to by Australia, stated that they 'reaffirmed climate change as the single greatest threat to the livelihoods, security and wellbeing of the peoples of the Pacific...'[32] But, behind the scenes, Australia insisted on the removal from the statement of references to transitioning away from coal as an energy source, sparking an angry response from Pacific island leaders.[33] Even a rhetorical commitment to meaningful action on global warming is anathema to Australia, committed as it is to defending the domestic fossil fuel industry. Deputy Prime Minister Michael McCormack dismissed concerns over the future of the Pacific nations because of climate change, saying: 'They'll continue to survive because many of their workers come here and pick our fruit...grown with hard Australian enterprise and endeavour and we welcome them and we always will.'[34] In the late 19th century, Australian colonialists tapped Pacific islands for indentured labourers; for McCormack, these nations' existence can again be reduced to a source of cheap labour for Australian agriculture.

Climate change is not the only element adding unpredictability to regional international dynamics. At the time of writing, the COVID-19 pandemic was in full force, adding to diplomatic tensions between China, the US and Australia. It is unclear how long it will take to bring the pandemic itself under control. But its impact in triggering the most severe economic crisis globally since the 1930s will be felt for years. In their post-Cold War euphoria, the prophets of neoliberalism declared that globalised, free market capitalism would be accompanied by a mutually beneficial and peaceful international political order. The Marxist theory of imperialism points to a more troubled reality.[35] Capitalism is a fundamentally crisis-ridden and competitive social system. When nation states seek to contain these trends within their borders, they displace them into the international sphere. So, the result of global economic crisis will not be international cooperation for recovery, but intensified competition and conflict between states trying to defend the specific interests of their capitalist classes.

This does not mean that the US and China will inevitably be drawn into open warfare on the scale seen in the World Wars, given the enormous risks and costs entailed for both parties. But nor can this prospect be entirely dismissed. And the more likely prospect of lower level or regional conflicts is terrifying enough. True, the Australian state is not looking to start a war. On the contrary, as the powers benefiting from the current regional order, both Australia and the US will attempt to avoid any upheaval of the status quo. They will portray themselves as the champions of 'stability' and 'international rule of law.' This is in keeping with the longstanding pattern of Australian imperialism presenting itself as purely 'defensive' in nature. Such posturing is given credibility by the undeniable crimes of the despotic Chinese regime, today committed in the first place against its own citizens in Hong Kong, Xinjiang and Tibet.

In this respect, O'Lincoln's book *Australia's Pacific War* is recommended as a supplement to the current work.[36] It shows how the logic of imperialism as systemic competition between rival powers was responsible for World War II in the Asia-Pacific, rather than the supposedly unique aggression of Japan. In a period when militarism and international tensions are once again on the rise, maintaining a consistent internationalist political perspective will be increasingly difficult. Any such politics must be grounded in an understanding of Australia's own history, not as victim, but as agent of imperialism, which is O'Lincoln's central concern in *The Neighbour from Hell*.

Sam Pietsch, Canberra, October 2020

Robbers & spoilers

Soon, there would be nowhere to run. European empires, both colonial and informal, expanded steadily between the Napoleonic wars and World War I. Initially, this didn't even require a rabidly imperialist climate of opinion. Richard Cobden and John Bright, liberal leaders of the free-trade Manchester school, argued before the 1870s that Britain's prosperity didn't depend on directly possessing colonies. They believed that such places would do business with Britain in any case, while the mother country only incurred extra expense by having to defend its direct control. Oxford professor Goldwin Smith even called for withdrawal from the colonies.[37]

But these arguments were downplayed by successive governments. Bourgeois politicians have little use for economic theories unless they fit with pragmatic assumptions. Based on common sense, they expected intensified competition as Britain's industrial supremacy declined; and they looked to captive colonial markets as sources of raw materials and strategic strong points to protect them. Whatever the economics, it seemed to work. In the first half of the century, Britain acquired key trading posts in Singapore, Aden and Hong Kong, annexed New Zealand and Natal and steadily strengthened its position in India and Latin America. The two other major imperialist powers were France and Russia. Expansion was driven by several factors. The key underlying cause, however, was the rise of industrial capitalism in Europe. It created companies seeking raw materials; products and capital seeking outlets; and the military technology enabling small bands of soldiers to vanquish great armies, as mocked in *The Modern Traveler* by Hilaire Belloc:

> Whatever happens we have got
> The Maxim gun and they have not.[38]

In the second half of the century, as new players (Belgium, Germany, Japan, the US) entered the scene, the atmosphere thickened. In Britain, the Royal Colonial Institute emerged, Benjamin Disraeli made a pro-imperialist speech at the Crystal Palace, and the Imperial Federation League grew up in the 1880s. Meanwhile, the German *Kolonialverein* began lobbying for colonial expansion, as did Belgium's Crown Prince Leopold. The 1870s were a decade of preparation for an orgy of colonial expansion.

The race began in the eighties. In 1881, France established a protectorate at Tunis; during 1884-85, it did the same in Annam (Vietnam). The British military occupation of Egypt took place in 1882. By 1884, Germany had African colonies. From 1887, France began taking over a swathe of equatorial Africa. This process of expansion continued until World War I. European influences – political, military, economic and cultural – were imposed on every corner of the non-European world, on an unprecedented scale.[39] Massive brutality, theft and genocide were all part of the experience, and nowhere was this more true than for the Aboriginal and Torres Strait Islander people of Australia. The architect of British colonial policy in the south-west Pacific, J. G. Thurston, believed that the wrongs the Anglo-Australians had committed in the name of Christianity, civilisation and progress were manifold:

We are...a race of robbers and spoilers.[40]

Often, the most enthusiastic imperialists were the leaders of local settler populations. Their circumstances made them contemptuously indifferent to the fate of Indigenous people. The prospect of new territories nearby aroused their commercial hungers and political ambitions; and, conversely, they feared the consequences should some rival power establish itself in the region.

The key economic issues on the imperial frontiers were land and labour. Implanting capitalism required making land into a commodity, alongside the mobilisation of a labour force to extract wealth from the soil. From the exploitative perspective of British settlers, the people already living there were sometimes seen as a nuisance and sometimes an opportunity: a nuisance when they perversely resisted being driven off their land, but an opportunity if they could be put to work. Australian Aboriginal people resisted the logic of wage labour economics. Their system of 'socialism,' lamented a Queensland clergyman, 'hindered any improvement and rightful ownership.'[41] Blacks often proved difficult to turn into labourers, so labour had to be imported. Mostly, it came from the British Isles; but, in North Queensland, indentured labour arrived from the Pacific.

The Australian colonies displayed expansionist tendencies almost from the beginning. In order to segregate different groups of convicts and create places of secondary punishment, the authorities founded outstations soon after the initial settlement at Sydney Cove. In addition, the presence of imperial rivals prodded the colonists to grab new territory step by step. Reports of the Frenchman Freycinet's explorations, the foundation of Singapore and the growth of regional trade all drew the NSW Government's attention to northern Australia. Some voices demanded the establishment of a settlement at Swan River because the area was too strategically important to fall into French hands. In 1817, Governor Macquarie made it clear that no rival power would be permitted to establish bases anywhere on the continent.

However, the earliest expansionism flowed directly from British policy, not local initiative. In fact, there were local chauvinist voices in Sydney, such as W.C. Wentworth's *Australian* newspaper, which disliked the Colonial Office 'scattering British subjects along the coasts of New Holland...like so many bats in a forsaken dwelling' based on decisions by lieutenant dunderheads.[42] By the mid-1820s, the historic growth of the pastoral industry, which would so mercilessly drive the Indigenous people from the land, was already underway. A more sophisticated local economy emerged, accompanied by quasi-autonomous political structures. Yet, the process was still overwhelmingly driven by the dynamic of British capitalism: the wool industry would not have amounted to very much without the hunger of British textile mills for its products.

The rudiments of an Australian nation did not yet exist, and, from the vantage point of London, or even Sydney, the distinction between 'Australia' and elsewhere in the region was still fairly vague. New Zealand, New Guinea, Norfolk Island, even Fiji were placed in much the same category as, for example, Western Australia. They were all relatively close and were inhabited by 'savages' – in fact, the doctrine of *terra nullius* extended to New Guinea, which was its great misfortune. These were all inviting targets.

Sealers from NSW had established bases in New Zealand by 1791. A supply of flax and timber attracted traders, including members of the NSW Corps prepared, in historian E. J. Tapp's description, to go to almost any length to enrich themselves.[43] Governor King had ideas of importing Maori people to work as shepherds – the first hint of a labour trade. In 1814, New Zealand was treated to a visit from Samuel Marsden, at the head of the first missionary contingent.

Although both traders and missionaries initially preferred to keep government involvement to a minimum, they provoked enough local antagonism within a few years to need protection from redcoats. Merchants began calling for a military presence after Maori, angered by abuses from white sailors, massacred the crew of the *Boyd* in 1810. By 1823, the *Sydney Gazette* was already trumpeting plans for serious colonisation; and, in 1826, a group of merchants and shipowners in the whaling industry called for British intervention 'on commercial, humanitarian and strategic grounds.'[44] The argument for intervention was strengthened by the actions of adventurers selling firearms to Maori people and fomenting strife between them. These pressures gradually drove both the Sydney authorities and the Colonial Office to act.

In 1819, Governor Macquarie appointed the missionary John Butler as a JP in New Zealand. In 1832, the Colonial Office appointed a Resident. After attacks on the crew of the *Harriet* in 1834, Governor Bourke sent two ships with troops to take bloody vengeance. Towards the end of the 1830s, that prince of colonisation schemes, Edward Gibbon Wakefield, helped initiate the New Zealand Colonisation Company, which put further pressure on the government. In the same year, NSW Governor Gipps' mandate was enlarged to include New Zealand. Finally, a strong British force arrived in 1840 to impose terms on the Maori tribes at Waitangi.

Administrative links did not last long, but New Zealand remained an economic dependency of NSW for many years, so this is perhaps the first hint of an Australian imperialism. However, it was the 'long boom' after the 1850s gold rushes which consolidated Australia as a distinct centre of capital accumulation, with autonomous local ruling classes, elaborate machinery of state and a flowering of local expansionist sentiment.

The hungry eyes turned first to Fiji. In 1859, the NSW Legislative Assembly resolved that the island group should become a British possession. This was the first time an Australian legislature had tried to influence imperial foreign policy. This followed the Crimean War, which had created a scare about invading Russians and provoked greater interest in international affairs. However, interest subsided again until the late 1860s, which saw the 'Great Fiji Rush.' Destruction of cotton plantations during the American Civil War had caused a worldwide shortage of this crop, which grew readily in Fiji. The result was a flow of investment and settlers from Australia.

Enthusiasm was greatest in gold-rich and optimistic Victoria, where a wide range of business figures backed the Polynesia Company in late 1868. The company failed in the end, but it stimulated other, more successful firms. The most famous was the Melbourne-based CSR. In 1900, it would make investments worth over £2 million, was exporting 88 per cent of the islands' sugar and spirits and had imported tens of thousands of Indian labourers. The Melbourne *Age* drew political conclusions from the commercial trends, in an article that illustrated the sub-imperialist dynamic:

> The most prosperous colonies have been founded without the assistance of, frequently in direct antagonism to, the wishes of the parent State...if England refuses to interfere, Australia will do well to discuss the advantages or disadvantages of stepping into the breach...Since England can rule India, why should not Victoria make the experiment of trying to rule Fiji?[45]

Glib arguments for annexation were to hand: the settlers needed protection from local unrest, as did capital investment; and humanitarians could be assured that direct rule of the islands would stamp out the trade in Black labour. Efforts to promote British rule of Fiji continued in the 1870s, with the Polynesia Company making representations to both the Victorian and NSW governments, and two inter-colonial conferences taking up the issue.

Still, the issue didn't dominate Australian politics. When Britain finally raised the Union Jack in the island group in 1874, pressure from the antipodes was only a minor factor in the decision. The 1870s and even the early 1880s were primarily a period in which the key arguments for expansion in nearby islands were rehearsed and lessons learnt from early mistakes. For example, advocates of annexation had generally resisted suggestions that the Australian colonies should shoulder the expense of administering the new territories, an attitude which irritated London. This mistake wasn't repeated in the 1880s, when Australia finally managed to join the race to divide the world.

A variety of colonial interests favoured imperial expansion in the Pacific. If we simplify the pattern slightly, we can identify each with one or another of the three eastern colonies.

Gold-rich *Victoria* had surplus capital looking for outlets. Its industrial and political leaders were generally recent migrants with an international outlook. The dominant economic philosophy, protectionism, could be readily extended to the idea of protecting investment abroad and forestalling rivals like the French through state intervention. Victoria was also the main base for the nationalist Australian Natives Association and for the Presbyterian Church, which had a lot of missionaries in the islands and demanded imperial intervention to bolster their position. Premier James Service was both a Presbyterian and a committed imperialist, as was a later premier from the other side of parliament, James Munro.

The bible bashers presented their cause as humanitarian, but they were not averse to using force to establish themselves; in any case, they tended to bring an imperial military presence in their wake. Reflecting on the New Zealand experience, a Maori prophet later described the missionaries as a sheath for the Pakeha (European) sword:

> These men showed us this beautiful scabbard, all adorned with gold and jewels...and then came a man in a red coat...and all of a sudden drew a sword out of it, and cut off our heads.[46]

The missionaries campaigned for suppression of the labour trade. While this had its humanitarian side, it was also motivated by self interest. Extensive labour recruiting in the New Hebrides (now Vanuatu) destabilised the local society and thus made missionary work more difficult and dangerous. Instability also opened up potential opportunities for French intervention, which the Protestant missionaries feared.

New South Wales, by contrast, was a centre for traders who were much less concerned with annexation. Trade could flourish, regardless of who ruled the islands, and French settlement looked like an opportunity rather than a threat. Two leading politicians, Alexander Stuart and George Dibbs, were shipowners who grasped the fact that French-ruled New Caledonia accounted for nearly 40 per cent of all NSW trade with Pacific islands. NSW was a centre of free-trade ideology. It also had more Catholic voices, who generally welcomed the French presence.

Queensland was different again. Sugar planters in the north of the colony, which recorded the arrival of some 62,000 Pacific Islanders between 1863 and 1904, wanted Black labour and saw annexation as a means of getting more of it. The sugar industry was only profitable on the basis of cheap labour. Regulations supposedly intended to prevent abuses in this labour trade were something of a joke, since the trade 'was run for the planters, merchants and ship-owners who ran the colonial politicians and saw Queensland's development as the supreme good.'[47] Kidnapping, violence and sexual abuse were rife, and even many islanders who came voluntarily did not understand the terms or duration of their engagement. It was not until the early 1880s, after a number of scandals, that the politicians began to take the issue seriously. Meanwhile, however, Victorian-based missionaries and political liberals presented annexation precisely as a means for stamping out the labour trade, so a unified imperialist front between the two colonies was difficult to maintain.

There were some areas of common ground. One was hostility to the introduction of French convicts into the region. Having fought bitterly to end transportation to Australia, the colonists were not happy to see even small numbers of felons sent to New Caledonia from the 1850s. When larger numbers arrived in the 1870s, this became an important issue, especially because the French legislature was considering sending them to the New Hebrides as well. W. G. McMinn writes:

> The tendency to explain every case of washing stolen from a clothesline in terms of New Caledonia was temporary, but the affair had the permanent effect of sensitizing Australians and particularly their politicians to the 'problem' of European penetration of the Pacific.[48]

In addition, there was significant Victorian investment in Queensland and, therefore, some common commercial interests. This made it easier for the two colonies to stick together when it came to foreign policy.

Raising of British flag on New Guinea annexed by Queensland in 1883. Source Wikimedia

The frantic eighties

Australian expansionism in the Pacific reached its 19th century peak between 1883 and 1885. The main arenas were New Guinea and the New Hebrides.

Queensland Premier Thomas McIlwraith sent a small party, led by a police magistrate, to raise the British flag in Port Moresby in April 1883. McIlwraith, a Presbyterian like so many other keen imperialists, was not acting on British instructions. He had been alarmed by an editorial in the German *Allgemeine Zeitung* proposing German annexation of the non-Dutch eastern half of New Guinea; he had called on London to forestall this by an intervention of its own, indicating that his government would foot the bill. But he did not wait for a reply. Seizing on the presence of a German warship in the area as a convenient pretext, McIlwraith created a fait accompli.

The Queenslanders made several attempts at justification. The islanders had attacked a few white settlers; there was growing dissatisfaction with the colony's military posture; and steamer traffic in the Torres Strait was on the rise. The politicians carefully kept one other motivation in the background: the sugar planters' continuing search for labour. It was proving politically difficult to get 'coolies' from India, and existing sources in the Pacific were limited. A majority of the Queensland papers referred to this issue in March and April 1883. They tactfully stopped mentioning it after British missionaries and humanitarians started campaigning around the issue.

New Guinea had great appeal for budding imperialists. Like the Australian continent, it was regarded as *terra nullius*. This doctrine didn't deny the obvious presence of Indigenous people, relying on Locke's argument that rights to the land depended upon the application of labour to improve it.[49] Where tribal cultures could not satisfy this demand to the satisfaction of imperialists, they were considered fair game. In addition, local opinion saw New Guinea as belonging geographically to Australia, just as much as Tasmania. So it is not surprising that other premiers lined up with McIlwraith. So did *The Age*, which opposed the evils of the coloured labour trade but saw the issue primarily in strategic terms:

> it is at least as important to Australia that New Guinea should be annexed as it was that New Zealand should be secured. The

unappropriated parts of the world are rapidly being seized upon...England can afford to disregard the extension of French colonies in distant areas [but] our security is at stake. Sooner or later it must come to something like a Monroe doctrine for Australia; and we shall have to intimate unmistakably that no foreign annexations will be permitted in countries south of the [equatorial] line.[50]

The Colonial Office was initially receptive. Although the Permanent Under-Secretary, Robert Herbert (himself a former Queensland premier), recognised that the 'intention has apparently been to force the hand of H.M. Government,' he considered it necessary to accommodate what would be a unanimous clamour for annexation from the Australian colonies.[51] However, Prime Minister Gladstone was not enthusiastic. Queensland had a bad reputation for mistreatment of Aboriginal and Torres Strait Islander people; the Black labour trade was unpalatable; and the Foreign Office discounted talk of German colonial ambitions in the area. The government disallowed the Queensland annexation, although it did declare the eastern half of New Guinea to be within its sphere of influence.

McIlwraith's initiative had failed, but it had a catalytic impact on colonial public opinion. On 6 June, a deputation of church leaders and MPs called on James Service seeking support for the seizure of the New Hebrides. As well as being encouraged by the New Guinea venture, they were alarmed by the establishment of a New Caledonian-based French company which was buying up large tracts of land in the islands. Service and his Cabinet endorsed a somewhat scaled-down version of their proposal. Perhaps he shared the hopes of Presbyterian missionary Daniel Macdonald that the New Hebrides would become the Australian Indies, yielding cotton, coffee, coconut oil, sugar, spices and other tropical products in large amounts.[52]

In July, the Victorian parliament called for the annexation of both New Guinea and the islands between it and Fiji, expressing a willingness to pay its share of the costs. Two thousand citizens attended a public meeting supporting the initiative and heard the prominent liberal George Higginbotham present the other key argument for annexation, the threat of French convicts finding their way to Australia. The French had passed a 'recidivist' bill, suggesting that

20,000 felons might be transported to the South Pacific, and they talked of acquiring the New Hebrides for use as a penal settlement. At least 247 escaped convicts had found their way to Australia from New Caledonia in the previous decade; now, it seemed that the worst fears of the settlers might be realised.

Once again, the colonies presented a common front – but not for long. South Australia and Tasmania, which had no strong interest in the issue, soon dropped out of the alliance, as did free-trade NSW. Queensland's defection might, at first, appear more surprising. McIlwraith was under the impression, common at the time, that British annoyance at the extension of the agitation from New Guinea to the other islands was a factor in their rejection of his own New Guinea adventure. However, he was probably also sensitive to plans by missionaries to use annexation of the New Hebrides to suppress the Black labour trade.

Victoria charged ahead with 50 public meetings, with dozens of local councils and a range of other organisations rallying to the cause in 1883 and 1884. The colony was at its 19th century peak, imbued with both local chauvinism and the emergent continental nationalism. Sub-imperial expansion blended with the campaign for federation, whose fiercest champions were Victorian capital, Victorian politicians and the Melbourne-based Australian Natives Association. The 1883 inter-colonial convention focused mainly on these two issues. The colonists' watchword, James Service had told McIlwraith in a telegram shortly before the event, should be 'Federation and all the islands.'[53]

In 1884, this sustained agitation finally pushed Britain into hesitant motion. In May, Colonial Secretary Derby renewed a largely symbolic offer to provide a resident commissioner to New Guinea, although proposals to declare a protectorate over all of eastern New Guinea were postponed. Meanwhile, German traders in the area, alarmed by the Queensland proposal, were pressing Berlin to seize the initiative. By the time London agreed to declare a protectorate in August, the Germans were ready to seize the north-eastern section, and Britain was not prepared to confront them over the issue. New Guinea might loom large in Australian thinking, but British imperial strategy was more concerned with Egypt or India. To secure British interests in the Middle East, and to guarantee the carve-up of Africa negotiated at the 1884 Berlin conference, it was important to placate Germany.

Britain's declaration of a protectorate over only the south coast of New Guinea, followed by German annexation of the northeast, provoked outrage in Australia (though less so in NSW, where a minority welcomed the trading opportunities opened up by Germany's action). Thousands flocked to public meetings in Melbourne and Ballarat. Little could be done to change the situation in New Guinea, and public attention soon turned to the emerging hostilities in the Sudan. However, the British Government was now more sensitive to public opinion in the antipodes, if only because it might tip the balance in electoral politics at home. In March 1885, the parliamentary opposition seized on indiscreet suggestions from a government emissary that France might receive a free hand in the New Hebrides. In the ensuing uproar, the government was obliged to rule out such a concession without Australian consent. It was the first time that colonial opinion had so clearly influenced imperial policy.

The outcome of two years' agitation was a compromise. Britain had taken over part of New Guinea and would eventually hand control to Queensland. In return, the colonies accepted the need to pay some of the costs of expansion, and Queensland accepted in principle that the labour trade would eventually have to end. Its end came after federation, with a restructuring of the sugar industry, a sugar tariff to make the industry capable of paying 'white' wages, and the advent of a national White Australia policy.

Australian attention now turned finally to the New Hebrides. Initial European interest in these islands had centred on the sandalwood trade. After supplies ran out in the 1860s, the traders in Black labour filled the gap. In the 1870s, small numbers of planters arrived to plant cotton, while Presbyterian missionaries gained control of the southern part of the group – except for Tanna, where the local people put up stiff resistance. These missionaries, remembering their early expulsion from Tahiti, were haunted by fear of the French, especially after the latter moved into the neighbouring Loyalty Islands.

Subsequent years had seen the establishment of the Compagnie Calédonienne des Nouvelles-Hébrides, with the explicit aim of achieving French control. In 1887, alarmed missionaries persuaded the Victorian and NSW governments to subsidise shipping services. This was followed in 1889 by the emergence of the Australasian New Hebrides Company, whose Victorian backers included two government ministers and four other MPs, former premier James Service and leading merchants. James Burns and Robert Philp of Burns Philp were also involved.

The shareholders participated on political, more than economic, grounds; they did not expect to get all their money back. In addition to waging the trade battle, the Australasian New Hebrides Company actively encouraged Australian settlers. Within the context of an Anglo-French condominium in the islands, which grew increasingly amicable as the two powers drew together in response to the German threat, this economic struggle continued up to the first World War.

Imperial frictions

So, the 1880s had brought chastening experiences. Australasian colonists were already aware that the interests of the mother country didn't entirely match their own. The anti-imperial arguments of Goldwin Smith had aroused antipodean fears in the 1860s. But it came as a shock to learn that, even in the fervently imperialist eighties, local expansionist appetites were still not shared in London. In the British capital, quarrels over tiny Pacific islands appeared to be an irritant, jeopardising other policy goals. During the agitation over the New Hebrides, Lord Salisbury complained privately that the colonists were:

> the most unreasonable people I ever have heard or dreamt of.
> They want us to incur all the bloodshed, and the danger, and
> the stupendous cost of a war with France...for a group of islands
> which to us are as valueless as the South Pole.[54]

Australia dared not slacken its efforts. Its duty, Alfred Deakin had declared during the New Guinea debate, lay in a struggle:

> to revive the colonial policy of the days of Raleigh and Drake,
> and the traditions of Sir Henry Lawrence in India, and of General
> Gordon, alone today in Khartoum.[55]

Departure of the New South Wales contingent from Sydney for the Sudan c 1885. Artist unknown. Source: Australian War Memorial

Such efforts would be more effective, of course, if the colonists could secure additional leverage within the Empire. One way to do so was to participate in Britain's adventures in other parts of the globe, in the hope that this assistance would be reciprocated if Australia or its interests were threatened. As early as the late 1840s, troops had been sent from NSW to New Zealand to fight in the Maori wars, but these were British troops; in any case, it was still the local neighbourhood. The first major opportunity arose with Gordon's failed adventure in the Sudan.

News of the drunken adventurer's death reached Australia in February 1885, arousing jingoistic anger and a fresh round of public meetings. Local sentiment was fierce, because Britain's 'betrayal' of Gordon was seen as related to its reluctance to support adventures in the Pacific. When Britain announced that it would intervene in the Sudan, the NSW Government took quick advantage of the situation by offering troops for Kitchener's expeditionary force. Acting Premier William Dalley had a number of reasons for

Company of Victorian Mounted Rifles on manouevre Victoria 1889. Artist unknown.
Source: Australian War Memorial

his enthusiasm: he was looking for ways to ingratiate his government with London in order to better resist Victorian calls for federation; and he needed something to distract public opinion from a crisis in colonial finance. However, he also hoped that this assistance would make it easier, at some future date, to seek British backing for Australian interests.

Victoria, which had previously offered two gunboats, hurriedly made plans to send a naval brigade and mounted infantry. Britain accepted the NSW offer but declined that from Victoria. It was the first time that white colonial troops had travelled to reinforce the British army in another part of the world. Sir John Robertson spelt out the political logic: 'if we expect England to stand by us in any trouble we ought to stand by England in her troubles.'[56]

The Sudan crisis was also the first important occasion when military adventures in distant places were used to boost national sentiment. Naming streets after Gordon, putting up statues and mustering thousands of schoolchildren to sing patriotic songs was an exercise in Australian nationalism as well as imperial pride. Few, apart from a small anti-war minority, saw any contradiction between the two; more prevalent was the view of a NSW MLA that the fate of Australasia:

> might be settled in the Sudan, in Egypt, in Afghanistan, in Cape Colony, or in the English Channel. Let England be defeated and humiliated, no matter where, and the colonies would suffer for it.[57]

Beating up national chauvinism might also help consolidate social peace, particularly in Sydney, where class antagonisms were strongest. NSW Opposition member H. S. Badgery hoped that sending a contingent to the Sudan would 'cement the people in this community of all classes and creeds in one common feeling.'[58]

Service believed that the NSW initiative had precipitated Australia in one week 'from a geographical expression to a nation.' Even a leftish Victorian Liberal MP such as W. F. Walker, who opposed imperial policy and sympathised with the Sudanese, thought that nothing had ever done more to make Australia's name as a nation.[59] At the same time, the action helped nudge Britain towards seizing part of New Guinea. Lord Rosebery, soon to become Foreign Secretary, thought that Dalley had 'played a great card for Australia and the Empire.' Dalley thought that it would make the British Government more accommodating in future.[60]

When tension in Afghanistan diverted Britain's attention from the Sudan, NSW's Acting Premier promptly proposed sending the Sudan contingent to the Indian frontier. However, the Afghan crisis subsided, and they returned to Sydney. In 1879, South Australia offered to provide troops to serve with Imperial forces against the Zulus, but its offer was declined. If Australian troops didn't shed much blood in remote climes, it wasn't for want of trying.

Federation brought a renewed interest in local imperial expansion. While foreign policy would generally be left to London, the new Commonwealth Government received powers to deal with the Pacific islands and immediately assumed responsibility for New Guinea. This was the era of a 'new imperialism,' with all the key European powers grabbing territory. The US was also emerging as a major player, having taken several possessions, including the Philippines, from Spain in 1898. Australian patriots often saw the US as an example to be emulated. Within the British Empire, the Boer War turned this enthusiasm into a frenzy. Although the battlefields were far from Australia, there was a feeling that rival empires were becoming a general threat. Even the imperialist coalition put together in 1900 to suppress the Boxer Rebellion in China, in which Australian troops took part, raised the spectre of other coalitions and other conflicts which might jeopardise Australian interests.

The rights and wrongs of faraway conflicts didn't matter much. When the Boer War broke out, the Victorian Premier admitted that it was 'difficult for us to say what the merits of this question are' – but that hardly stopped him supporting the British side.[61] Here, at last, was an opportunity to get a real piece of the action. Sixteen thousand young men sailed off to kill and be killed, as Australian politicians seized another opportunity to take out an insurance policy with the Empire and to cultivate local nationalism in the run-up to federation:

> A nation is never a nation
> Worthy of pride or place
> Till the mothers have sent their firstborn
> To look death on the field in the face.[62]

The Australian colonies' own military efforts are only comprehensible in this imperial context. Of course, our armed forces always claim to exist for defence, although this country's history is remarkably devoid of actual foreign threats. Early NSW and Van Diemen's Land (now Tasmania) did not need defending from anybody; one officer told Commissioner J. T. Bigge that the danger from fraternisation between convicts and Irish soldiers was a greater threat than attacks by foreign powers.[63] The importance of invasion fears, from then to the present day, lies in creating an ideological basis for imperial expansion. Australia's imperial ambitions in the Pacific, writes Stuart Ward, 'flowed logically out of a perceived strategic vulnerability.'[64]

The first specifically Australian military forces appeared at the time of the Crimean War. Having first passed a Volunteer Act, under which several troop units took shape, the colony of Victoria decided to lash out and acquire a steam ship. Governor Hotham would not settle for a small boat to patrol Port Phillip Bay. He wanted a war steamer and got one: HMCS *Victoria*. It was supposed to be for defence, but there were soon foreign adventures. When fighting broke out between Maori people and British forces in 1860, the ship spent several months ferrying troops and supplies to New Zealand.

The Crimean conflict had brought the first of many war scares. These were generally inane and always passed fairly quickly; but, while they lasted, they were important in legitimising 'defence' efforts. Without a panic about Russian invaders, Hotham might never have obtained his ship. In 1876, the prospect of another war with Russia prompted Henry Parkes to call for a review of military issues, undertaken by Sir William Jervois with Lt-Colonel Peter Scratchley. Their first task was to persuade the colonists that they needed local defence. They couldn't make much of a case, however, since the colonies had little to fear but raids. Another review by Major General J. Bevan Edwards in 1887 recommended a coherent national military and was therefore politically significant in promoting federation, but it did not identify any actual threat to Australia. The Colonial Defence Committee in London declared: 'There is no British territory so little liable to aggression as that of Australia.'[65]

The local militarism was part of what, with no intentional irony, was called 'imperial defence'. In 1896, the Intercolonial Military Committee recommended:

> Instead of thinking in terms of the continent and Tasmania...the defence region of Australia be extended to include New Zealand, New Caledonia, the New Hebrides, New Guinea, and portions of Borneo and Java.[66]

The authorities focused on three locations where serious military precautions were needed: Thursday Island in the Torres Strait, King George Sound (WA) and Port Darwin. To name them is to show immediately how little this had to do with defending the mass of the Australian population.

Thursday Island was the gateway to New Guinea, a major shipping lane for Queensland trade, a base for missionary efforts and the source of gunboats to punish islanders who dared to attack white people. Both Thursday Island and King George Sound were important, as coaling stations, in maintaining British naval power. Port Darwin was the point where the telegraph cable linking Australia to Britain came ashore and also the terminus of a transcontinental railway. Military efforts were focused on securing the shipping and

ROBBERS & SPOILERS 35

Cannon Cooktown. The placard reads: 'On April 10th 1885 the Cooktown Council carried the following motion "A wire be sent to the premier in Brisbane requesting him to supply arms, ammunition and a competent officer to take charge of same, as the town is entirely unprotected against the threat of a Russian invasion." This gun (cast in 1803 in Carron Scotland) 3 cannonballs, 2 rifles and 1 officer were sent.' Photo: Janey Stone

Lt-Colonel Peter Scratchley. Photographer unknown. Source Wikimedia

communications through which both Britain and the Australian colonies projected power.

This doesn't mean that the military had no domestic role. Scratchley cited the army's intervention during industrial disputes in Newcastle and Hobart and referred to 'the importance of having such a trained body to back up the police force in the event of civil disturbances.'[67] Just such a requirement arose in the early 1890s, when the Queensland Government deployed troops against striking shearers. Unpaid volunteer regiments were largely drawn from the middle classes and did not resist being used against workers. Another type of armed force, the Native Police, was used against the Aboriginal people. Whether on or offshore, the military existed not to defend the common people, but to secure conditions for capital accumulation.

Colonial ideas

Just as the interplay between Britain and several distinct colonial settler populations in the South Pacific was complex and contradictory, so too was the ideological framework which supported and, at the same time, reflected the various interests involved. Nationalism and racism have been the main components of most, if not all, modern imperialist ideology, and this was true in colonial Australia. But neither was simple.

The local nationalism began to emerge in the second half of the 19th century. For most people, it was still firmly located within a wider British or 'empire' patriotism. This was not surprising. The colonists might resent Britain's lack of enthusiasm for adventures in the Pacific, but they were not themselves oppressed by imperialism. On the contrary, even such nationalist writers as Ken Buckley and Ted Wheelwright contend that Australia overall benefited from relation with Britain, in increased production and better living standards.[68]

The logic of colonial nationalism made it hard even for those who might oppose one of Britain's imperial campaigns to do so consistently. During the Boer War, a minority of Australians opposed the British war effort and sympathised with the enemy, who fought better than expected. However, that sentiment could be easily deflected into the emerging cult of 'The Coming Man,' which celebrated the virtues of manly colonial fighters; this, in turn, became the basis of a new enthusiasm for white settlers everywhere taking

38 THE NEIGHBOUR FROM HELL

British and Australian officers in South Africa during the Boer War 1889.
Source: Australian War Memorial

up the 'white man's burden.' In other cases, anti-imperialism was simply xenophobic. William Lane's racism was part of a general desire to keep the rest of the world out of Australia:

> We want to be left alone. We don't care whether Canada loses her fishing monopoly or not; or whether Russian civil servants replace the British pauper aristocracy in Hindustan offices; or whether China takes missionaries and opium-dealers together and sends them packing; or whether the sun sets on the British drum beat or not – so long as the said drum beat keeps away from our shores.[69]

The actual nationalist element within this xenophobia was fairly uncertain, or Lane would never have left the country to found a utopian colony in Paraguay. When accused of deserting Australia, he replied: 'It is not a local question, not a national question, but a life question.'⁷⁰ Paraguay, it seemed, was an even better place to be left alone. This mentality effectively left imperialism unchallenged.

The second plank of imperialist ideology was racism. This was contradictory. On the one hand, a belief in the superiority of Europeans went logically together with imperial expansion. On the other, prejudice at home sometimes fed hostility to particular imperialist projects.

Hostility to the labour trade in the Pacific islands was partly humanitarian in nature but was partly based on racist hostility to the introduction of Black labour into Australia. Later, the *Worker*, paper of the Australian Workers' Union, argued that it was a simple matter to 'see through the plot of the Jew capitalists' which lay behind the Boer War. Henry Lawson warned that the Australian troops in South Africa faced the danger of 'niggers' crawling into their tents at night to 'rip out your innards.'⁷¹ Indeed, there was a strong racist streak in arguments both for and against the war:

> Pro-Boers felt that that most cherished ideal [White Australia] was violated by a war which was engineered by financial interests to secure an assured supply of cheap labour for the mines – black, brown, yellow or depressed white...Supporters of the war simply dismissed this interpretation and construed their own support as a premium to insure the inviolability of White Australia...when Chinese coolies were imported into the Transvaal in 1904 the critics crowed and the Australian Imperialists denounced their betrayal.⁷²

Since most critics of imperialism shared its fundamental nationalist and racist assumptions, it was easy for them to eventually embrace its strategic logic. Lawson had shared most progressive people's sympathy with the Boers, but, by the time of the 1905 Russo-Japanese war, he saw Russia as the champion of the white races in 'the struggle of the East against the West' and effectively defended Britain's Indian empire in 'the fearful war of races.'⁷³

Imperialist racism had direct connections to race conflict in Australia.⁷⁴ Palmerston's British Government fell against the background of the second 'Opium War,' and the ensuing election was dominated by hysterical rhetoric about alleged Chinese atrocities. Coverage of these developments reached the colonies in May 1857, contributing to a wave of local agitation that culminated in the Buckland riots.

Nationalism and white supremacy were also closely linked to the sexual politics of the era. Alongside the virile 'Coming Man' was an image of the ideal white woman as the lynchpin of family life, reproducer of the race and guardian of its purity. British and Australian colonists took this very seriously in places like Fiji, 'where the maintenance of minority power and status was seen to depend on racial purity' and 'where the *white* woman was unquestionably the protector of the *white* home.'[75] There, European women were under great pressure to bear numerous children, and their ability to work was even more limited than it was in Britain or Australia, because white prestige would be undermined if they did physical labour. Sexual morality was also particularly stifling for white women; they were expected to provide a sharp contrast to their 'native' counterparts, who were portrayed as morally lax.

From whatever angle we look, one thing is evident: from 1788, white Australia was not a victim of imperialism. Our rulers have always taken their place among the robbers and spoilers.

Two world wars and neo-colonialism

The first half of the 20th Century reshaped the global social order – and, with it, Australia. The patterns of our imperialism during this era deserve a substantial discussion in their own right. I try to provide this in my book, *Australia's Pacific War*,[76] and that discussion is too detailed to repeat. What this book can do is offer some additional insights based on the experience of the main colonised populations to our immediate north. The World Wars showed that, firstly, despite an occasional taste for fatuous peace-loving rhetoric, this country was an aggressive player in its region; secondly, that Australia could prepare itself effectively to fight, particularly by playing the race card and by using its industry to supply the battlefield. This country was never really on the defensive in either war, so it was well placed to assert its aggressive self in the region as hostilities came to an end. This is clear from statements by the Australian commander Thomas Blamey. Critics have asked whether Blamey's later offensives in the islands had any point to them, given that they contributed little to defeating Japan. But they had two purposes. One was to strengthen Canberra's strategic position; the other was to consolidate the position of other local imperialists, especially the Dutch in Indonesia. Blamey had warned:

> Were we to wait until Japan was finally crushed, it would be said that the Americans…were responsible for the final liberation of natives in Australian territories, with the inevitable result that our prestige both abroad and in the eyes of the natives would suffer much harm.[77]

The wars gave rise to the main post-war global imperialist trend, which has since consolidated itself and is commonly called 'neo-colonialism'. This means provision of formal or seeming independence alongside realities of continuing control, or supporting a country's independence on paper with the same ends in mind. The West generally was offering decolonisation to the Third World, but for their own reasons. Neo-colonialism was first developed by the US under the rubric of the 'Open Door' and seems to have been publicly given its modern name by the African leader Kwame Nkrumah in 1965.[78] The US approach reflected the belief that, if trade controls could be lifted, the US economy – with its greater productivity – could dislodge previous imperial rulers. Of course, the 'Open Door' was utterly hypocritical. The US embassy in London conceded in 1945:

> Sheer intellectual honesty compels us to say that the US favours multilateralism and non-discrimination in areas where we are in a strong competitive position; but resorts to subsidies, protectionism and discrimination in those areas where we are competitively weak.[79]

Hypocritical though it be, neo-colonialism had worked fairly well for the US when applied in the aftermath of the war. It hadn't worked so well for Canberra, but Australia was in a weak position, regardless of strategy. Certainly, ALP Foreign Minister H. V. Evatt hadn't been shy about his own expansionism. He planned not only to maintain control of Papua New Guinea, following World War II, but to extend Australian possessions in Indonesia at the expense of the Dutch, as is discussed below.[80]

Papua New Guinea

Australia came out of World War I in control of former German New Guinea, via the instrument of a League of Nations Mandate. To more fully exploit what is now called Papua New Guinea had been a long-term aspiration; wartime national leader Billy Hughes declared openly that these island were 'to all intents and purposes part of Australia.'[81] That wasn't just a matter of national pride: Deputy Prime Minister Joseph Cook hoped that the territory would be full of resources, perhaps including oil. To be sure, Canberra also claimed to be assuming responsibilities. In Senator Matthew Reid's magnanimous words, Australia must treat local people 'like grown-up children.'[82] Even on the most generous interpretation, this didn't mean much; it appears that conditions deteriorated after the Australian takeover.

Reforming German administrators had made some improvements to the condition of local people in the pre-war years. These seem to have gone backwards under the Australians.[83] Pacific historian Derryck Scarr records that the:

> often callow Australian servicemen who ruled the former German New Guinea from 1914–1921 were able to flog freely, just as their own concept of military justice allowed them to shoot pretty much at random when whites were killed by New Guineans.[84]

After 1921, the administration still took a 'permissive view' towards punishment and was freer with hangings than the Papuan Government.[85]

If the lash was one way to assert power, property management was another, probably more effective over time. Consider the case of Marist Brothers missionaries who bought land on Bougainville, but soon discovered the local people had no intention of accepting the transactions. The bible bashers had to call in gunboats to enforce their title. Years later, when the Forest Department wanted to exploit timber resources around Tonolei Harbour, local owners sought to lease the land but declined to sell; so land was expropriated. As a result of such methods, society polarised against the authorities. PNG became a land in which, according to historian Douglas Oliver, some police might be less disliked, some less liked, but all were more or less feared.[86]

Still, some Black people in the territory came out of World War II with hopes for a better future, expecting compensation from the whites for past exploitation. Such hopes were the basis for some of the social movements known as cargo cults among villagers overawed by the immense resources of the US war machine and then taken aback by its disappearance.

Australian possession of Papua New Guinea became a stepping stone to claims in West Papua. The latter territory, wrote the Department of External Affairs, was part of New Guinea since West Papua had been 'included in the Australian declared Pacific Security Zone in 1944.'[87] Australians' capacity for militarism manifested itself after the onset of a general Japanese defeat. Australian commander Thomas Blamey steadfastly resisted attempts to reassert civilian rule. The period of military rule that followed was used to plan post-war development. It was, Blamey declared, 'one of those rare moments in history when morality coincides with expediency.'[88] If nothing else, the military establishment understood expediency.

Indonesia

This emerging nation's independence movement seized the opportunity of the war and Japanese occupation to lay the basis for a full scale rebellion when Japan surrendered. It wasn't a great success militarily; but, with the rise of an independent Asia across the hemisphere, denying Indonesia *merdeka* (freedom) became politically impossible. Some Indonesians are under the impression that the Australian Government made a substantial contribution to their independence. This probably results from hearing the true story about genuine trade union support. That was impressive:

> The Australian Waterside Workers Federation (WWF) prevented Dutch ships laden with troops, munitions, and other supplies from leaving Australian ports. Starting in Brisbane, the embargo soon attracted wide support from workers in other major Australian ports including Sydney, Melbourne, and Adelaide. The WWF began by refusing to load Dutch cargoes and repair Dutch ships, and later boycotted all Dutch transport, stores, and depots ashore. The embargo continued until 1948. Thirty-one Australian trade unions and four Asian trade unions directly immobilized 559 ships that were supposed to supply the Dutch effort.[89]

Many Indonesians seem to have confused this with the cautious, hedged and belated help provided by the government (i.e. Labor, not labour). It's a confusion Canberra is content to leave undisturbed.

Until the war ended, it was firm Australian policy to restore Dutch rule, a stance backed up with material aid and armed force. Australian troops forced the independence forces underground for a time in the eastern islands,

Graffiti by Australian wharfies supporting Indonesia against the Dutch. Sources: Noel Butlin Archives Centre/Australian National University and Australian National Maritime Museum

46   THE NEIGHBOUR FROM HELL

Indonesian seaman speaking at pro-Indonesian rally Sydney. Daily Telegraph 29 September 1945. Source: Australian National Maritime Museum

making it possible for the butcher Paul Westerling to secure Dutch control. In early 1946, the USSR and Ukraine called for a United Nations enquiry into the Indonesian situation, aiming to put pressure on the Dutch. The Australian Government opposed it, as interfering in internal Dutch affairs. When Sukarno demanded an enquiry, Canberra was silent. In 1947, convinced that Australian strategic and economic interests required endorsing emerging national forces across Asia, the Chifley government moved towards a pro-independence stance in Indonesia. Now Evatt did want the case brought before the Security Council, because they were concerned not to miss opportunities.

Canberra Times 8 November 1945 courtesy Trove

'Surrounded as we are by non-Europeans,' explained Chifley, 'Australia could not be seen to be inactive.' [90]

Australian working class protest actions, pressure from troops wanting to go home, the needs of business groups, the diplomatic spotlight and perhaps Evatt's personality generated a certain erratic quality in Australia's Indonesia policy. On a visit to Washington, Evatt proposed 'that Australia assume postwar control of Dutch Timor, West New Guinea, and the Kei, Aru and Tanimbar islands'. On another occasion, he proposed a condominium, but governed by Australia. Once the hopes of grabbing territory had been dashed, Evatt concentrated on economic opportunities and political arrangements that would maximise them. He made it clear that Australia would be interested in expanding its economic relationships with its near neighbours in the Southwest Pacific, while Queen Wilhelmina proposed to revamp the Dutch empire to make it consistent with the Atlantic Charter.[91] Everybody was flexible. The essential point for us is that Canberra pragmatically followed its own interests, which pointed relentlessly towards Indonesian independence.

Finally, World War II had a considerable impact on the awareness of Aboriginal and Torres Strait Islander people about the wider world, and also on white people who came into contact with them. Black Australians had played a highly diverse role in the war and came away with greatly enhanced confidence. Many whites conversely became aware of the apartheid conditions under which Indigenous people lived. One consequence was a series of strikes across the north of the continent, supported by Australian communists – including well-known figures such as Frank Hardy and Don McLeod. Strikes in the immediate post-war years foreshadowed later actions, including dramatic struggles over land rights.[92]

Riders on the storm

World War II sealed Britain's decline, while opening the way for an 'American Century'; at the same time, Australia inevitably reoriented from London to Washington. At first glance, the turning point seems to be Labor PM John Curtin's 1941 declaration that 'Australia looks to America, free of any pangs as to our traditional links or kinship with the United Kingdom.'[93] However, this statement shouldn't be seen in isolation. It contrasted with Curtin's speech to the 1943 ALP Federal Conference predicting a fourth [British] Empire after the war.[94] And, in fact, the first 10 or 12 post-war years witnessed a reaffirmation of Australia's position within the Empire. Imperial sentiment was only a secondary factor in this; much more important was the trade position. The Korean War wool boom apart, the economic profile of the US in Australia was much lower than Britain's, and this material factor ensured that other linkages with Britain retained their importance for a decade. Intelligence collaboration between the various English-speaking countries continued intensively.[95]

Should we celebrate or regret continuing British links? It depends on whose nuclear nightmare you prefer. The three governments – UK, US and Australian – strengthened their grip on advanced nuclear weapon technology. Scientific prodigy Marcus Oliphant had close links to the British scientific establishment, from which he drew inside information about Britain's own nuclear program early in the war. He passed the details on to senior diplomat and Cabinet minister Richard Casey and so to the Australian Government. It was Canberra that initiated a new project to build a bomb, but British and Australians were driven by the same frustrations. The US wanted to maintain a nuclear monopoly; and neither Australia nor the UK seemed to have the capacity to develop nuclear weapons alone. Eventually, a return to British–US collaboration abruptly ended the main aspects of the UK–Australia project. Britain dumped Australia from the nuclear game, and that was that. This prodded Canberra to look more closely at the US connection.[96]

US strategy had prioritised Europe and the Middle East, with the Korean conflict seen as an anomaly. Canberra offered the 'Australian territory' of Manus Island (part of Papua New Guinea) to the US as a military base, but this aroused little interest. At first, Washington also showed little enthusiasm for an Asia-Pacific security pact. However, Communist successes in Asia began to focus minds in both Washington and Canberra. Since British power was clearly in decline east of Suez, entrenching Australian interests in Asia required a strengthened US alliance; and, with France losing an Asian empire at Dien Bien Phu, there was realistically no way that the US would hold back from trying to pacify Southeast Asia. The Chifley government had shown little desire to play a direct role in Asia beyond 'Anzam' (Australia, New Zealand, Malaya), but this changed under the Menzies administration.

Canberra scrapped commitments in the Middle East in favour of the Commonwealth Strategic Reserve Centres in Malaya, becoming a founder of the US-oriented South East Asia Treaty Organisation. Both the Centres and SEATO were ineffectual; their importance lay in signalling a change in orientation. The ANZUS treaty dated to 1951 and was potentially far more important, but its actual implications were unclear throughout the post-war period. The history of post-war Australia–US relations can be read as a continual testing of the treaty.

There was, of course, a substantial common ideology between Washington and Canberra. The US was immersed in anti-Communist scares, and Menzies promoted his own. Consider the timing of the 1955 dispatch of troops to Malaya to suppress Communist insurgents. This came within roughly the same two years as the French defeat at Vietnamese Communist hands, the aftermath of the Petrov spy scandal and the anti-Communist split in the ALP. An anti-red psychosis accompanied the provision of troops to Vietnam, illustrated by Brigadier Stuart Graham's tantrum with a staff member in Vietnam: 'Communism is evil! Communism is bad! You are a serving officer and you have no right to think anything else.'[97]

But common ground didn't prevent tensions. The US complained of a maddening Australian aggressiveness. The US State Department thought that Foreign Minister[98] Percy Spender's interest in a Pacific treaty was less about a guarantee of Australian security than access to allied decision-making machinery, while Secretary of State Dean Acheson thought that the Australians' most cherished idea was to have a 'direct and permanent relationship between their chiefs of staff and ours,' a fixation which became an 'embarrassing problem.'[99] When a subsequent Secretary of State, Dean Rusk, visited Canberra in May 1962, Foreign Minister Garfield Barwick 'interrogated' him in a way that 'visibly irritated the American and startled the New Zealanders present.'[100] Far from being a slave to Washington, Canberra jostled for an expanded influence.

The common ground betrayed differing agenda. Each time the US pressed Australia to commit more forces to US adventures, Canberra performed a balancing act. Richard Casey's memoirs explain that there was a desire to minimise the drain on resources, but also a desire not to appear to be penny-pinching or stalling. Similarly, one could disagree with the US, but preferably not in public. Casey felt that Washington was aware of what a small military Australia maintained. For an ally constantly pestering the US to do things, the Australian imperialists didn't contribute much themselves, which was embarrassing. Perhaps one ought to do more, Casey thought. Yet, in Cabinet, he stood against those who would follow the US 'whatever they did.'[101] He believed that the pros and cons must all be carefully calculated, even if some of them counted against Washington. Here we have neither a conventional picture of the US charging headlong into war, nor one of Australian politicians crawling to the US. Instead, there was cynical calculation on both sides, and not for the last time. Five decades later, Paul Kelly would write:

> For half a century the Australian way of war has been obvious: it is a clever, cynical, calculated, modest series of contributions as part of US-led coalitions in which Americans bore the main burden. This technique reveals a junior partner skilled in utilising the great and powerful in its own interest while imposing firm limits upon its own sacrifices.[102]

US General Van Fleet (far left) inspects Australian troops in Korea.
Source: Australian War Memorial

Every military scheme was for 'defence'. But a key element was 'forward defence,' sending troops far to the north to fight people who had never dreamed of invading us. Key documents show no meaningful threat to Australia. That is, while there were threats to Australia's ability to exploit the world market, there was no military threat to people living on this continent. An internal government analysis of Australia's strategic position from 1946 dismissed the major powers as being benign or lacking the power to attack. Russia was a 'potential enemy of the future,' but even that country couldn't mount more than raids on the Australian continent. Likewise, a 1953 document dismissed actual defence of the Australian continent as presenting 'a comparatively small problem.' When Australian strategists spoke of defence, they meant protecting 'Australia's interests,' which tended to mean overseas investments, assets, revenues and trade links. A military raised only to defend Australia, Menzies jibed, would be like a 'wooden gun.' It was in this context that Canberra desired to 'take responsibility' for a strategic zone to the north and east.[103]

To stop countries falling to the Communists, which could tip their riches into the hands of rivals, Australian 'diggers' invaded these countries. And to persuade the public that there was an actual danger, the 'domino theory' argued that the fall of one pro-Western state would bring down another. Spender offered this argument immediately after the North Korean attack in 1950. It would be used many times after that.

'Burn out the place' – Korea

At the end of the Second World War, Korea was split in two. Although the Soviets arrived in Korea a month earlier than US troops, they still honoured an agreement to divide the country at the 38th parallel. North of that line, the USSR was in control; below it, the US reigned. Australians played a certain role – not a very good one – in the southern capital, Seoul.

The pushy Australians had got hold of Britain's seat in the UN Temporary Commission on Korea, which gave Canberra a certain influence on US policy and also on the political scene in Seoul, where they had an office. They found the South Korean capital a turbulent place, ruled by the US, the police and extreme right wing elements led by Syngman Rhee. During elections in 1948, Australian diplomats on the spot reported intimidation by right wingers and police, who seized newspapers and engaged in such violence that all the political parties except the far right boycotted the election.

Prisons were more crowded with political activists than under Japanese rule, and one US observer was kept awake at nights by the screams of tortured prisoners. Generally, however, the US intelligence service G-2 was too preoccupied with suppressing the left to enquire closely into the methods of its Korean collaborators.[104] The Australian Labor government could have made high-profile international protests about these crimes, but it did not.

Apart from politicians' hostility toward specific aspects of Japanese politics, following World War II, the overall Australian diplomatic stance towards northeast Asia had been vaguely left-liberal in character.[105] Following a lead from Foreign Minister H. V. Evatt, diplomats and analysts associated with external affairs secretary John Burton resisted the cruder anti-Communist and pro-Rhee attitudes coming out of Washington. This attitude was reflected in the frank assessments about Rhee from diplomats in Seoul in the immediate pre-war years. Australia didn't fully line up with the US' diplomatic position in Korea until Menzies' conservatives won government in 1949. We might perceive a simple contrast between Labor and Liberal, with Labor as inherently more progressive. In reality, the changes in Australian policy began under Chifley. Burton moved to a position closer to the US in mid-1948; Evatt made his shift to the right some time before the 1949 poll. Labor politicians and diplomats were responding to right wing pressures mounting in Australian society.[106]

The oppressive right wing climate was also felt at the Australian grassroots, making it difficult to organise opposition to the war. Communist-led unions carried motions, and the Seamen's Union tried to create momentum for workers banning war shipments, but without much success. The Australian Peace Council pulled together a network of 'peace parsons' and held sizeable meetings, but it was harder to mobilise against the actual war in Korea than around general sentiments. The Council could draw 10,000 to hear the Red Dean of Canterbury two months before the war began but couldn't repeat this later, when it really mattered. There are reports of two small demonstrations, one by students.[107]

Rhee won the 1948 poll; but by 1949, opposition was growing and insurgents were challenging the government. Australian observer A. B. Jamieson conceded that the regime's legitimacy relied on the authority of a police state; he had personally rescued two journalists from the more gruesome types of torture. Thirty candidates had been arrested, and 5,000 people were in long-term detention without trial. These new outrages didn't prevent Canberra from recognising the 'Republic of Korea' (South Korea).[108] The level of discontent did, however, embolden the 'Democratic People's Republic of Korea' (North Korea) to invade the south. The invasion was the beginning of a catastrophe for the Korean people, but it created salivating opportunities for the Australian Government, and Foreign Minister Percy Spender eagerly cabled Menzies in London about seizing them:

> I feel very strongly that we must give some immediate response... My appreciation of the military position in Korea is that the US, though not prepared to admit it, is in a very difficult if not desperate position...any additional aid we can give to the US now, small though it may be, will repay us in the future one hundred fold.[109]

The military impact might be slight, he added, but it could have considerable political impact. On the other hand, to hold back could cost 'an opportunity of cementing friendship with the US which may not easily present itself again.' Menzies was overseas, hard to reach, and known to oppose any such ventures. Neither did he share Spender's enthusiasm for a formal alliance with the US. But when it became clear that Britain would send troops to Korea, acting PM Artie Fadden agreed to do the same, making a point of dispatching forces before London did. Acheson and Truman signalled their pleasure by facilitating a large World Bank loan to build infrastructure in Australia. This sounds like surprising generosity from Uncle Sam, but the infrastructure would enhance Australian military power, contributing to a stronger alliance.

With the advent of the Cold War, US policy towards Japan had become less punitive towards the Japanese establishment (but more punitive towards the left) and much more focused on rapid economic development. Japan was to be a prosperous, right wing ally. Australia, still trading in paranoia about Japan, disliked the changes and demanded security guarantees. It was hard for Washington to oppose a Pacific security treaty when Spender put direct pressure on US presidential adviser John Foster Dulles and even on President Truman himself. Spender suggested that the conversation with Dulles had been the 'discussion from which the present framework of security in the Pacific stemmed.' That is, Australian initiatives rather than pressure from Washington had laid the basis for the ANZUS treaty.[110] It was a concession the US made to win acceptance of their Japan policy and in exchange for Australia joining the war.

For the war, Australia provided the No. 77 Squadron of the RAAF and a battalion of ground troops. The Australian troops, writes John Hooker, 'had no idea that they were to be involved in one of the dirtiest wars in history.'[111] Neither side was innocent, but it's clear that most of the mayhem came from the Western allies, for the simple reason that only the Western side had the capacity to drop 550 tons of incendiary bombs on the city of Sinuiju alone and 'remove it from the map' in Bruce Cumings' words; or to follow up a week later by blanketing the town of Hoeryong with napalm to 'burn out the place.' By 1952, as a result of the Western onslaught:

Just about everything in northern central Korea was completely levelled. What was left of the population survived in caves, the North Koreans creating an entire life underground.[112]

No war crimes on the northern side matched the August 1950 Daejon massacre by Syngmann Rhee's forces, which killed 5,000–7,000 civilians. The only thing in doubt, write historians Stewart Lone and Gavan McCormack, is whether US agents were directly involved.[113] That Western soldiers, including Australians, committed smaller scale war crimes is apparently not in doubt.[114]

The fortunes of war were uncertain. A northern offensive nearly drove the southern forces into the sea, but General Macarthur turned the tide with his Inchon landing. It appeared that the northern forces would be wiped out. However, MacArthur and his 'favourite fascist' General Willoughby underestimated the capability of Asian fighters.[115] Chinese forces drove MacArthur back, and the final outcome was a ceasefire at the 38th parallel. It was a 'draw,' but widely seen as a Chinese victory.

The Malayan 'emergency'

The most important Asian conflict through the fifties was the Malayan 'emergency.' This had roots in post-war grievances, such as those of rural Chinese squatters who had trouble getting permanent residency. The squatters saw themselves as making an important contribution to Malayan society, given that they brought into use sizeable tracts of previously empty land and forest. They felt slighted, and their difficult circumstances led to unrest. The British authorities resorted to repression, not as badly as Syngman Rhee, but cruelly nonetheless.

The emergency also had roots in British–Australian plans to establish a new state where the conservative Malay sultans would have the most clout. To clear the way for this, the imperialists set out to smash the left. The campaign against the left emerged slowly and unevenly, reflecting the contradictions of the immediate post-war situation, before the Cold War began and while Communists were still allies. A Communist guerrilla unit joined the victory parade in London, and the Pan Malayan Federation of Trade Unions flourished. But, by 1948, the colonial government had launched an anti-union drive, cheered on by the employers who demanded 'death, banishment and particularly flogging.' Much was at stake: Malayan rubber was the Empire's biggest foreign exchange earner.[116]

As early as October 1945, government troops fired on a demonstration in the Chinese village of Sungai Sipit, in Perak. Perak was an urbanised area, centred on Ipoh. In June 1948, the authorities began destroying 'illegal' crops; in retaliation, Communists killed three managers of a farm. In the same month, the union federation was banned. By August, 4,000 people had been arrested, and by October some hundreds more, as villagers in Perak were prosecuted and saw their homes destroyed by troops. They fled to the town. A prolonged guerrilla war began.

It was a disaster for the left; yet, at the outset, there were hopeful signs. The Communists were popular for challenging the power of gangs which exploited farmers, and their politics had some resonance. An April 1948 peasant conference in heavily Malay Kedah discussed the widespread evictions of farmers and declared: 'Our greatest enemies are the capitalists.'[117] Another plus was Washington's clear signal that it would not intervene in Malaya, barring extreme circumstances. But ethnic and other divisions in the working class and the populace generally sealed the Communists' fate.

Australia sent an infantry battalion along with RAAF aircraft and personnel, artillery and engineers. A construction squadron built a runway for the Butterworth air force base. RAN ships fired on Communist positions. But there were other forms of attack. On 11 December 1948, a patrol of Scots Guards surrounded and entered the village of Batang Kali, Selangor, where they separated the male villagers from the others. That evening, one of the men was shot, and the next day, another 23. The Foreign Office and Defence Ministry have long insisted that they were shot while trying to escape. But some of the Scots Guards published accounts in the 1970s that disputed the official version. An eyewitness remembered watching as the men were shot.[118]

The term 'emergency' was used to save the colonists money; but it was a civil war, with roots in World War II. When news of it reached Australia, veteran Ken Harrison remembered the militia he had campaigned with against the Japanese, and he decided not to forward information to help the Malayan authorities find them. He thought of the smiling young men and the risks they took for the Australians. He remembered how shabbily the militia and villagers were treated in return:

> I thought of how 'military requirements' had caused us to burn down the Chinese village of Jemaluang in January 1942. We had watched dozens of Chinese families trudge past our gun pit carrying all that they possessed and with the black smoke of their homes hanging ominously above them...later some of those who had been our friends must have had bitter thoughts about the destruction of their homes, particularly as Jemaluang was neither attacked nor defended.[119]

To suppress the rebellion, the British used a ruthless counter-insurgency strategy known as the Briggs Plan. The cornerstone was forced relocation of around 500,000 rural dwellers – 400,000 of them Chinese – from villages on the edge of forests into guarded camps called 'new villages.' Deprived of contact with their popular support base, the militia were defeated.

Malayan precedents were important for Menzies' Vietnam War. A Cabinet minute linked the two explicitly. When the government faced warnings from 'peace parsons' about the risks of war with Indonesia, it pointed to success in Malaya.

Some of the same tactics would be employed again in Vietnam, but without much success, because there were important differences between the two wars. China and the USSR provided ample support, delivered across borders which the US was unable to seal. At its height, the Malayan insurgent militia had some 8,000 fighters, compared with 100,000 Viet Cong guerrilla fighters in South Vietnam and 250,000 soldiers in the North Vietnamese military. The Vietnamese were relatively united on a national basis, whereas the people of Malaya were not; Malays and Chinese, in particular, were often at loggerheads, but the Chinese also had divided allegiances between the Guomindang nationalists and the Communists.

It was the lack of a revolutionary political party capable of uniting the country's ethnic groups that ensured defeat. The Communists made valuable efforts along these lines, but these were ultimately limited by their nationalist approach. The success of Britain and the Malay right wing in launching a

Ethnic Chinese-Malay civilians forced to relocate due to the Briggs' Plan. Note the British soldiers surrounding them and the emaciated physique of the civilians.
Source: UK Imperial War Museum

pro-Western nation (Malaysia) undercut the patriotic politics of the Malayan left and was seen across Asia as countering the Western weaknesses exposed in Korea. The spotlight now shifted to Indonesia.

Indonesia confronts the West

Indonesia's independence movement was primarily led by mainstream nationalists such as Sukarno, rather than the Communist Party (PKI). This, in turn, made it easier for Washington to apply a 'neo-colonial' approach, backing Indonesian independence as a way to displace the Dutch. In West Papua, ethnically and socially very different to the Malay populations, the Dutch were able to hang on for longer by posing as sympathetic to Papuan independence. Both Jakarta and Washington were determined to nudge the

Dutch out as Washington worked to improve relations with Jakarta. Canberra, on the other hand, loathed the prospect of an Indonesian takeover on 'its' borders, because of its own ambitions for the territory.

The US attempted to tame Indonesia by backing the provincial rebellions of 1957–58. US officials were tipped off about these rebellions by their Australian counterparts. No doubt motivated by a desire to place oil companies like Caltex beyond Sukarno's reach, the US supplied the rebels with money, arms, ammunition and even personnel. CIA pilots dropped supplies to the rebels and bombed government forces. US Secretary of State John Foster Dulles publicly backed the insurgents and moved the US 7th Fleet to Singapore. But the revolts fizzled out, and the US concluded that it had to live with the Sukarno regime in Jakarta – indeed, to indulge it to a point, for fear Sukarno would turn to Moscow or Beijing.

As in Malaya, much natural wealth was at stake. Indonesia produced 40 per cent of the world's natural rubber, 20 per cent of its tin and a huge array of other resources, including oil and precious metals. Japan, the main industrial economy in the Western-fostered alliance in Asia, imported most of its oil from Indonesia. The island nation sat astride major sea routes, giving it a strategic importance to match its economic profile. Provoked by working class agitation and plant seizures, Sukarno had seized Dutch assets during the fifties, and he was under constant pressure from the PKI for further radical steps.

Given the determined efforts Soviet and Chinese representatives were making to build influence in the country, it isn't hard to see why the US wanted to stay on friendly terms with Sukarno. (So, for that matter, did Australia – Indonesia and Malaya were the main recipients of Australian aid under the Colombo Plan.) There were divisions in both Canberra and Washington about how to deal with Indonesia's claims on West Papua; ultimately, it came down to the Australians seeing the prospect of an Indonesian takeover as a challenge to their island mini-empire centred on Papua New Guinea, and a more general fear by Australian authorities that Indonesia sought 'regional hegemony.'[120] On the other hand, Robert Komer of the National Security Council spoke for many US leaders when he said that a pro-Communist Indonesia was a greater worry than whether Sukarno controlled 'a few thousand square miles of cannibal land.'[121]

The US enabled Sukarno to secure West Papua for Indonesia, but the frantic, counterpoised diplomatic activity by the Dutch and Australians achieved little. Eventually, the United Nations would preside over a bogus 'Act of Free Choice' in which repression by the Indonesian forces ensured that 1,025 delegates voted unanimously to join Indonesia. In this situation, Canberra showed itself to be a team player for imperialism. The Australian Government forcibly prevented two Papuan leaders from travelling to the UN by jailing them when they reached Papua New Guinea; and it played a leading role in getting the UN General Assembly to accept the 'Act of Free Choice' without debate. UN officials, cited in a secret US document given to Australia, said that almost all Papuans wanted independence. When it was denied, Australia's ambassador to Indonesia, Gordon Jockel, found the mass of Papuans 'sullen and discontented.'[122]

Canberra was sullen for different reasons. In Australia's most important regional crisis since World War II, the US alliance had proved less useful than was hoped. Canberra concluded that it needed to get closer to the US leaders and try more aggressively to shape US policy. Vietnam would soon provide an opportunity. For the time being, Australian interest remained focused on Indonesia, led by the charismatic but chaotic Sukarno, and the British administration in Malaya, along with its local supporters.

Having defeated Australia over West Papua, Sukarno harboured other expansionist designs focused on British colonies in the Malay world. Having contained the emergency, the British proposed to establish a post-colonial state embracing Malaya, Singapore and North Borneo. It would be called Malaysia. The plan relied on juggling population balances between heavily Chinese Singapore and Malay-related ethnic groups in Borneo, to ensure a Malay majority. This proved unnecessary, because Lee Kuan Yew took Singapore out of the deal. Even with a clear Malay majority, however, Malaysia was a threat to Sukarno's ambitious plans to unite the region against Western imperialism. Under the slogan 'crush Malaysia,' he declared plans for confrontation (*konfrontasi*).

The conflict sharpened after the December 1962 Brunei rebellion. It was sparked by the People's Party, which opposed federation. When this party took up arms, the Sultan called for British troops from Singapore to suppress the uprising. Australia provided aircraft to the British force.[123]

On the other side, there was some indication that the Indonesians helped the rebels. In early 1963, Indonesia launched a series of cross-border raids into Malaysian territory. The government was under considerable pressure from below, as worker supporters of the PKI seized British firms and demanded nationalisation.[124]

April 1963 saw the first clash of Australian troops with Indonesian infiltrators in Sarawak. Over the following two years, alongside Britain, New Zealand and the US, Australia struggled to find diplomatic and military responses that would secure the new Malaysian federation while not antagonising Sukarno and propelling him into the arms of the Soviet Union. The undeclared war ran alongside a curious sort of conciliation. For example, in March–July 1965, Australian troops killed 30 Indonesian soldiers, and an SAS squadron was in the field. Yet, Australia continued foreign aid payments to Jakarta. Western aid and training were being channelled to the pro-Western Indonesian military, who would soon be ready to strike against the country's president.

Despite posturing from Sukarno and alarmist chatter in Canberra, nobody really thought that Indonesia could win the confrontation militarily. However, the West could suffer political defeats. To Canberra's dismay, Britain was steadily losing interest in sustaining the remnants of empire east of Suez. Indonesian Foreign Minister Subandrio remarked pointedly to Australian diplomat Ed Shann that a war would end British influence in South East Asia, and that this was the Indonesian objective. Shann did not dissent.[125] Washington was worried that a disproportionate response to *konfrontasi* might push Sukarno into the arms of the Soviets, so the delicate US and Australian manoeuvres continued. When Jakarta placed stricter regulation on US firms, President Kennedy offered a deal. When Sukarno seized British companies and cut diplomatic ties to Singapore in September, Washington suspended arms shipments, but that was all.

Australia's traditional backers, the British, were gradually being pushed out of their central role in Asia, and the US showed little interest in Canberra's plans to clip Sukarno's wings. The ANZUS treaty seemed to be of limited use in informal conflict. A secret 1963 memorandum between Washington and Canberra said that key passages in the treaty 'related only to overt attacks and not to subversion, guerrilla warfare or indirect aggression.' It added that 'any US forces would be air and sea forces, plus logistic support.' But, without ground troops, a US intervention wasn't much use.[126] Menzies might have called it a wooden gun.

So Australia had to make a substantial contribution. Canberra sent not only its usual battalion of infantry, but also two squadrons of the Special Air Service, a signals troop, artillery and engineers. Ships and RAAF squadrons also took part.

The balance sheet of US-Indonesian relations, from West Papua through *konfrontasi*, showed that the US, being further from the action and with an eye on the global picture, was more willing to accommodate Sukarno than were the Australians. Moreover, Washington refused to make the public military commitments Canberra so desperately desired. In the subtle game of trying to get as much out of the US with the smallest contribution by Australia, the Menzies government had botched it. That would need to be fixed by paying some dues in Indochina.

The US tended to see Indochina as the source of (mostly Communist) 'threats.' For reasons of proximity, Australia was more worried about Indonesia, which was painted as a threat by public statements out of Canberra, although internal Australian Government documents described its military as 'badly equipped and ineffective.'[127] These contradictions ceased to matter when a 1965 coup by the Indonesian military eliminated the PKI from the political map and largely isolated Sukarno. A CIA assessment described the post-coup massacres as among the worst mass murders of the century. The CIA's own hands weren't clean either.[128] During the 1965 crisis, the CIA supplied arms and other help specifically earmarked for use against the PKI. Brad Simpson of Princeton University describes the CIA as 'directly involved to the extent that they provided the Indonesian armed forces with assistance that they introduced to help facilitate the mass killings.'[129] The US Government also provided the names of thousands of PKI leaders to the Indonesian army, which hunted them down and killed them.[130] The fact that such stories took many years to come out appears to confirm US diplomat Marshall Green's smug 1965 prediction that risks of exposing US culpability were 'as minimal as any black bag operation can be.'[131]

Australian Treasurer Harold Holt gloated: 'With 500,000 to one million Communist sympathizers knocked off, I think it is safe to assume a reorientation [in Indonesia] has taken place.'[132] Indonesia would cause the West no more bad dreams; the US and its allies could focus on Indochina. Observers have suggested that, with the fall of Sukarno and the PKI, the logic of Australia's Vietnam policy should have changed. The key argument for backing the US in Indochina, notes Peter Edwards, was:

> to be confident of American military support if confrontation were to develop into a major conflict. [The Indonesian] events undermined much of the rationale for the Vietnam commitment.[133]

But that is to forget the more general lessons arising out of events before the coup (including *konfrontasi* and West Papua): that Washington didn't seem to be sufficiently committed in Asia, or to backing Australia at key junctures. Menzies would search in vain for a solution in Vietnam.

Vietnam: yanked into war?

The 1954 Geneva Conference had called for a temporary division of Vietnam, with elections to be held in 1956.[134] But the US blocked the elections because the Communists, being better campaigners and ballot-stuffers, would have won them. Ngo Dinh Diem and his cronies then won a fraudulent vote in the south, and he became president. The Communists formed the National Liberation Front of South Vietnam, or Viet Cong. Under Eisenhower, the US kept its involvement in the continuing conflicts to a minimum, leaving the Saigon regime to 'sink or swim with Ngo Dinh Diem.'[135] After 1960, President Kennedy took a more interventionist approach: Diem was bumped off, as was Kennedy in time. Kennedy's replacement, Lyndon Johnson, was cautious about committing ground forces but, after winning the 1964 elections as a peace candidate, he used a probably faked incident in the Gulf of Tonkin to secure Congressional backing for a massive intervention.

In 1968, Johnson came unstuck. North Vietnamese and Viet Cong fighters staged the spectacular Tet Offensive, challenging US forces all over South Vietnam. This had a devastating impact on US public opinion. Reports of the massacre of Vietnamese civilians at My Lai, dissent at home and an informal but massive rebellion in army ranks led by discontented Black GIs sealed a

US defeat. But, earlier in the decade, the Western powers had still hoped that sheer firepower could bring them victory.

In announcing the dispatch of an Australian battalion to Vietnam, Bob Menzies had declared the Western invasion of that country a great moral action. The Australian left saw the troops' departure very differently. A Brisbane leaflet charged: 'We are fighting for the sake of American imperialism. Our diggers die for dollars.' Labor Senate leader Murphy said that Australians were involved because the US Government decided they should be, while the Sydney Trade Union Moratorium Committee argued:

> the powerful and enormously rich families who own American monopolies see to it by lobbying, bribery and corruption, that the war in Vietnam continues and escalates to the extent that they secure the maximum in profits from war contracts.[136]

The left saw the US as dragging the country into war.

Neither scenario fitted the facts. Budding Prime Minister Harold Holt touched on the real situation: the core objective was locking the US into a deeper Asian commitment. Winning in Vietnam was secondary, and safeguarding democracy came a dismal last. Echoing Dennis Warner, Holt told diarist and minister Peter Howson that, since the USA was now committed for the long haul, 'we will win there and get protection in the South Pacific for a very small insurance premium.' Howson himself remarked that a US commitment in Asia meant protection for the Australian state. General John Wilton, chair of the Chiefs of Staff Committee, spoke as if answering the standard leftist critique: 'it wasn't a question of us being dragged in by the USA, it was us wanting to have the USA dragged in.'[137]

The US had hesitated to get deeply involved in Vietnam, because it feared the political dangers of a major war in which its allies would be few and their contribution token. Despite US wariness, that is pretty much what happened. Only the South Koreans made a significant military contribution. Between 1965 and 1973, some 313,000 South Koreans fought in Vietnam. By contrast, from when the first advisers arrived in 1962, just under 60,000 Australians, including ground troops and air force and navy personnel, participated in

Vietnam. However, the Koreans were effectively mercenaries, receiving significant pay from Uncle Sam.

Still, Australia's 60,000 figure was considerably higher than the number who joined the Korean, Malayan or *konfrontasi* hostilities. To lock in a certain level of US commitment, Canberra was now prepared to pay a political price by providing more troops, resulting in casualties and unrest over conscription. But sustaining the war effort despite these problems posed additional challenges. One challenge was convincing ordinary Australians that they faced a tangible threat. On 29 April 1965, when Menzies announced plans to send a battalion to Vietnam, he claimed that 'the takeover of South Vietnam would be a direct military threat to Australia.' His Chiefs of Staff had said nothing about this menace, and Peter Howson wrote that such a threat remained 'remote till at least 1970.'[138] Actually, a look at the map showed how unlikely it was that Viet Cong would land at Bondi. The real danger on the government's mind was a US withdrawal from Asia.

Australian efforts to deepen Washington's engagement in Asia gained traction only slowly. By 1964, the only way forward seemed to be persuading the US to escalate, then win, the Vietnam War; and Australia would have to provide some of the additional troops in order to be credible in US eyes. Canberra seems to have prepared a diplomatic offensive around this agenda, to be launched as soon as President Johnson won re-election in November 1964. Foreign minister Paul Hasluck arrived in the US capital on 21 November 1964 to pursue the war-hawk agenda, as did Defence minister Shane Paltridge. Howson arrived a few days later with the same message. Johnson was still cautious, but Howson was pleased to get a 'ready ear' from the air force chief, General Curtis LeMay. LeMay was the architect of unspeakable US fire-bombings over Japanese and Korean cities; while he denied proposing to bomb North Vietnam 'back into the stone age,' those who knew him found such language characteristic.[139] This was apparently the type of mover and shaker Menzies wanted to encourage.

In late 1964 and early 1965, US war planning centred on a two-phase escalation of the war. Phase One was a slight intensification, planned to run for a month and followed by Phase Two. But Johnson was so nervous that Phase One dragged on. At this point, a secret interdepartmental meeting recommended that Australia take the lead and press the US to move to Phase

Two. 'For the first time the Australian government had decided it must openly and actively attempt to change the direction of America's Vietnam policy.'[140] In point of fact, writes diplomat Malcolm Booker, 'it was the Australian government which in the early part of 1965 pressed on the American government the need for strong military action in Vietnam.'[141]

When Menzies announced commitment of a battalion to Vietnam, he chose his words carefully. He said that Australia was 'in receipt of a request' from the government of South Vietnam for further military assistance. So it was. He had a letter from the South Vietnamese Prime Minister accepting 'the Australian government's offer' and requesting 'dispatch of the force.'[142] So he dispatched it. This glossed over the ambiguities of the request from Saigon and the degree of arm-twisting that Washington and Canberra had to undertake. Until shortly before Menzies' announcement, there was still doubt about whether Saigon would approve a role for Australian troops. Probably, it only acquiesced under heavy pressure. On the other hand, Menzies was utterly keen, later saying that his government had been 'looking for a way in, not a way out.'[143] It was the first war Australia fought without any British involvement.

Did the ALP oppose the war? Yes and no. ALP leader Arthur Calwell had an anti-war reputation, and he campaigned against aspects of the war in the 1966 election. But just as Labor had shown itself capable of a pro-war stance in the run-up to the Korean conflict, the same applied in the mid-sixties. Calwell tried to balance between his pro-war deputy Gough Whitlam and the genuine anti-war figure Jim Cairns for as long as possible. Calwell said that the US must not be forced out from Vietnam, while Whitlam thought that US motives in South Vietnam were 'above dispute.'[144] Only after Menzies wedged him by announcing troops for Vietnam did Calwell make a major speech critical of the war. When Labor suffered electoral defeat in 1966, Whitlam set about pulling the party back to the right. Not until public opinion turned decisively against the war did the ALP do the same.

One way to present Australia's boutique imperialism as superior to the crass US stuff is to promote its supposed humanitarian virtues, declaring that, as an editorial in *The Australian* has claimed, 'our military has earned a reputation for compassion.'[145] But even if Australian troops in Vietnam committed no My Lais, still there is more to be said. To begin with, the main culprits of

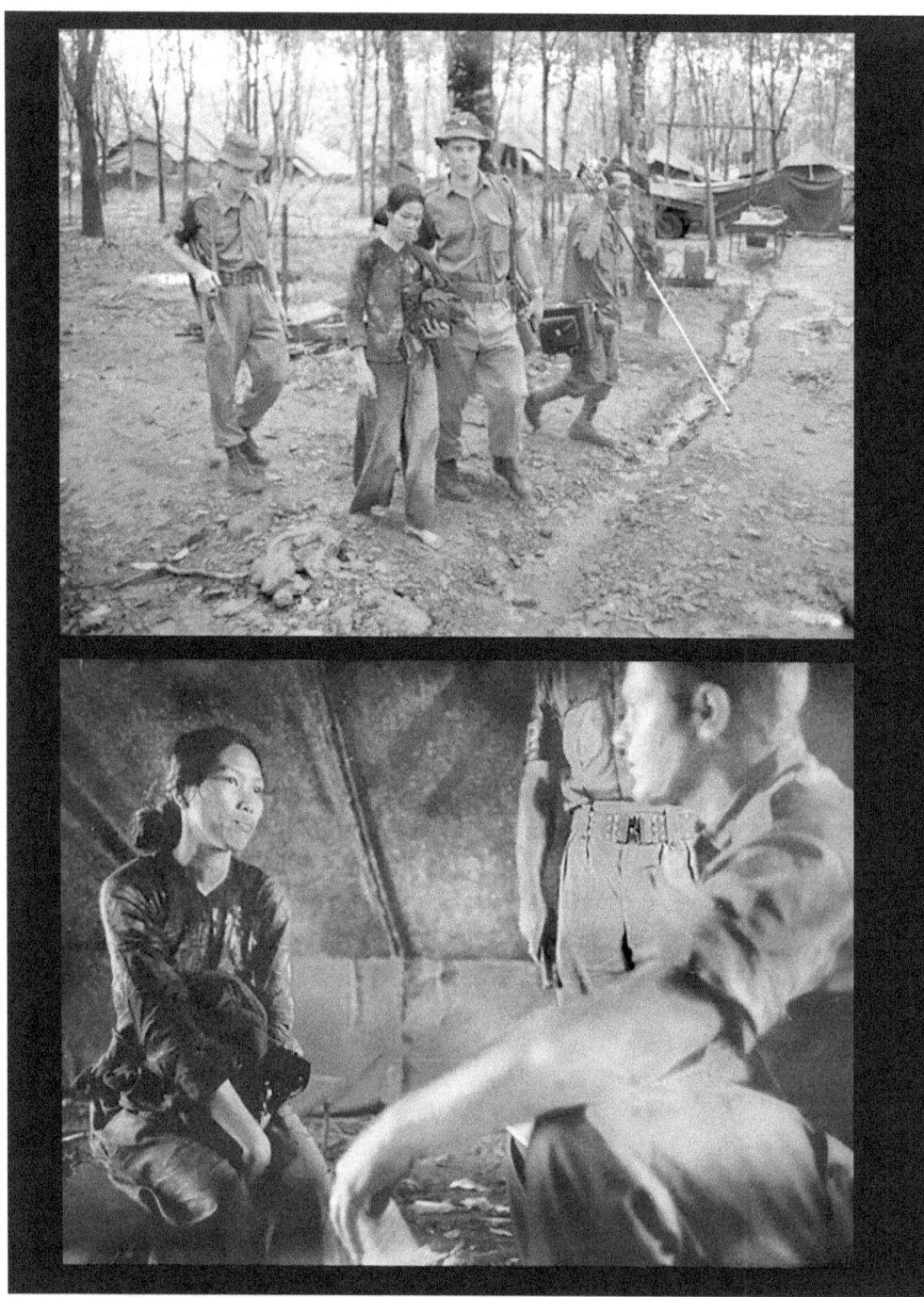

To Thi Nau, a 23 year old NLF woman, was captured in the Nui Dinh Hills with a radio. An Australian division intelligence unit interrogated her in a tent at the 1st Australian Task Force Base, subjecting her to waterboarding in the process. The photos show her being taken to the base by soldiers, part of the interrogation and subsequently being blindfolded for transportation. Although the photos don't themselves show the torture they were central to what became known as the "water torture case". Photos: Gabe Carpay. Source: Australian War Memorial.

wartime atrocities were not the frontline soldiers, but the leaders in Canberra and their associates in the Australian ruling class who encouraged and apologised for the genocidal US war effort. No amount of restraint by frontline troops compensated for that.

Even where the Australians behaved better towards the local people, it didn't change the reactionary logic of the war. Brigadier Stuart Graham tried to move away from the US approach, summed up in the mission statement for Operation Cedar Falls, which was a bald 'Kill VC'. Graham drafted a new mission statement for his troops which amounted to protecting the people from the enemy. The trouble with this was that the people *were the enemy*. And so, when Private Paul Murphy recalled another relocation exercise, he could say: 'They hated us...Old ladies were crying and wailing; they'd just been thrown out of their ancestral homes.' Yet he could add that 'militarily there was a justification for it.'[146] The abuses of war were not an optional extra.

And they did commit conventional atrocities. Their first resettling of villagers involved bombings and the destruction of the traditional village. Other documented cases include the shooting of wounded Viet Cong, the dragging of Vietnamese corpses behind armoured vehicles and the waterboarding of a young woman – the last accusation long denied but finally confirmed by an SAS sergeant who had been there.[147] Finally, there are Stuart Rintoul's interviews, which confirmed the general climate of fear:

> you could see the fear in the faces of the old people. You'd kick a door down and there would be an old man and an old lady huddled up in the corner...[148]

Was all this necessary to defend the Australian people? Hardly. No threats confronted you and me as a result of defeat in Vietnam. 'The Prime Minister had tacitly acknowledged the fading relevance of forward defence against falling dominoes,' writes Paul Ham about the post-Vietnam situation. 'China, steeped in domestic crises, was no longer considered a regional threat, and the Soviet Union preferred not to upset its delicate co-existence with the USA.'[149] Australia remained aggressive because it was imperialist. Indeed, growing public awareness of these issues became an increasing obstacle for Canberra and ultimately contributed to its defeat – not just in the immediate military sense, but also because a mass anti-war movement had flow-on effects in terms of other radical movements, such as Aboriginal and Torres Strait Islander campaigns which won historic land rights victories in the 1960s and 70s.

The Vietnam defeat resulted in precisely the US retreat from Asia which Canberra feared. Far from playing the obsequious lap dog, Australian Foreign Minister Andrew Peacock wrote a pointed 5,000-word message to his US counterpart Cyrus Vance complaining that the steadfast image of the US had been badly damaged, and calling on the US to maintain a strategic presence in the region.[150]

To be sure, the post-World War II imperial balance sheet for East Asia was more even overall. In South Korea, a military embarrassment was giving way to economic boom. The Malaysian project had succeeded, despite some racial tensions, and Indonesia was in the hands of its bloodstained anti-Communist military. Measured against the objectives set in the 1950s, Australian policy seemed a modest, if morbid, success. One fundamental challenge remained unmet: how to ensure a substantial US commitment to back Australia's imperial interests in the Asia-Pacific. A solid victory in Vietnam would have improved the State Department's perceptions about Asia and perhaps made them happier warmongers, with an ongoing enthusiasm for the region. The struggles of the Vietnamese, together with civilian protests in the West and rebellion in the US military, shattered that hope.

Testing the Vietnam Syndrome

The US and Australian governments had both needed to win in Vietnam. But they were thrashed; and, after the defeat, the US had to retreat. At the cost of some loss of credibility, President Nixon withdrew from aspects of the US 'security' role in the Asia-Pacific. His so-called 'Nixon Doctrine' also dictated that the US shoulder a greater part of the cost of their 'defence.' This could open up new opportunities for Australian war industries, but at a cost. Its ideological counterpart was a complex of ideas and sentiment against any more foreign wars, known as the Vietnam Syndrome. Military doctrines can change fairly rapidly; but popular anti-war sentiment can run very deep.

Sections of the left hoped that political independence might flow from developing the capacity to produce weapons in this country and from putting more Australian boots on the ground. But this prospect has little attraction for any ruling class not anticipating a war; attaining self-sufficiency in arms production and troop deployment is more expensive than delegating 'defence' needs to the US. The idea did, however, gain some traction between 1965 and 1990, when dissident analysts such as Des Ball and Paul Dibb argued that defence needs could be based on 'national and regional concerns' rather than 'intervening in faraway wars.' Dibb was even appointed to write a 1986 report to government arguing for a shift in this direction.[151] Later, Ball took a strong stance against the 1991 Gulf War, partly because this same Dibb report was being abandoned. So there was a vaguely leftist trend, but it remained patriotic in tenor.

Dibb and Ball won a hearing for their self-sufficiency plans because they weren't just spinning utopian fantasies. The currency of these ideas resulted from the eclipse of Britain east of Suez and from the US defeat in Vietnam. In the short term, they suggested a way to save money at a time when the global economy was in a parlous state. So Dibb found temporary acceptance for his ideas.[152]

All things being equal, it's certainly better to reduce our involvement with the US empire. Moreover, a debate on self-reliance can open a wider discussion about why this country meddles in other people's affairs. But all things are seldom equal; in the political climate of the seventies, for Australia to have taken the path of self-sufficiency led by Gough Whitlam and Malcolm Fraser would have meant developing a stronger military-industrial complex, with all its costs. While the high point of the military self-sufficiency doctrine was noteworthy in the history of the liberal left, it was quickly forgotten during the Gulf War fever of 1990–91. Policy papers from the Medical Association for Prevention of War represent a continuation of the Dibb–Ball tradition – but with less emphasis on pulling the military back to a continental position, and more emphasis on 'good regional citizenship' issues such as human rights and climate change.[153]

More recent Australian policy in the Pacific fitted neatly with the militarist paradigm pursued by the US. Canberra has emphasised the dangers of 'failed states' which shelter insurgent groups and drug cartels – all of which fits with the US wars on terror and drugs. This is reinforced through support for neoliberal free-trade orthodoxy and by moves to increase labour mobility. In fact, this country, with its relatively large economy and military, has been effectively recognised by US strategists as the regional 'police.'[154] From the 1990s, it has confronted a series of crisis factors in both fields, to some effect. Some of the region's problems derive from a breakdown of the large-ish public sector the colonial powers left behind and the subsequent imposition of neoliberalism by the likes of the World Bank.

The 1997–98 Asian economic crisis provoked a flight of capital to the Asian mainland, causing internal, and sharpening external, political tensions. The fallout was most notable in the Solomon Islands, where a withdrawal of Malaysian capital triggered ethnic conflicts, a series of coups and the 2002 Australia–New Zealand intervention. But oil was still profitable. To keep an eye on it, BHP's Jakarta representative, Peter Cockcroft, paid a clandestine visit to jailed East Timor insurgent leader Xanana Gusmao a year before Timorese independence.[155]

East Timor crisis and after

The 1999 Australian invasion of East Timor capped a new round of upheavals. This, too, had its roots primarily in the Asian economic crunch, which brought down the Suharto dictatorship and opened a path to East Timorese independence. Canberra found that its preferred plan for Timorese stability – rely on Suharto – was no longer viable. John Howard reluctantly fell back on his second option, which was to send in the Australian military. This brought him great success, not only on the battlefield but in politics. For once, he secured support from the broad Australian left; they not only accepted, but demanded, that the troops go in, in the hope of saving lives.

Howard's difficulties were with the USA. Having backed US adventures in the Gulf, Canberra expected prompt US backing for the 1999 invasion of East Timor. Initially, however, Washington showed little interest. When Howard asked Bill Clinton for a military contribution, the President said that he couldn't send ground troops. That was galling, especially because Howard had readily contributed to Operation Desert Fox, Clinton's 1998 attack on Iraq. It took determined lobbying in Washington before a US naval vessel with a contingent of marines arrived to show the flag.[156]

Clinton's reluctance reflected US awareness of the Vietnam Syndrome. This sensitivity was also strong in Australia, but it declined sharply after the invasion of East Timor, when support grew for overseas interventions by the ADF. A gloating editorial in the *Financial Review* ridiculed those who had thought that the only legitimate role for the Australian forces was to defend Australian territory:

> The calls for action in Timor are ironic because many of those who fostered the political climate in which the army was run down were the loudest in demanding Australia intervene there.[157]

John Howard also seized on the popularity of the Timor action to rehabilitate the Vietnam War by presiding over dozens of farewells and welcome-homes for the forces, something allegedly denied to Vietnam veterans in their day.[158] The war itself was also rehabilitated through the star-status of 'Vietnam hero' Major General Peter Cosgrove.[159] Cosgrove led the invasion and became a celebrity.[160]

East Timor 1999: Were Australian troops sent to save lives?

This is documented from two published sources, but I take all responsibility for the conclusions. James Dunn puts firm dates against the worst killings.[161] Australian troops arrived in Dili on 20 September and in the provinces some time after that. Dunn offers the following dates:

- In **Suai**, the worst massacre was on 6 September.
- In **Dili**, the latest date he can confirm is also 6 September.
- In **Maliana**, the main massacre was on 8 September.
- In **Lautem**, he confirms a date of 25 September, resulting in nine deaths – horrible enough, but not a large enough number to change the general picture, which is that the worst killing seems to have happened by 8 September. This was before Indonesian leaders Habibie and Wiranto announced (on 12 September) that they would accept peacekeepers, and well before the troops arrived.
- Even in **Oecussi**, Dunn says, 'the main killings occurred on 8, 9, and 10 September.' Oecussi is an enclave surrounded by Indonesian territory, where Australian troops didn't arrive until 2 October. If there was any place the Indonesians and their militia could have committed full scale genocide well after the ballot, this was it. Yet Dunn's account suggests that the worst violence subsided before Howard committed the troops.

The Commission for Reception, Truth and Reconciliation reported in 2005.[161] The Commission's dates for major massacres are somewhat different but broadly consistent with Dunn's, except that they do show more significant violence in Oecussi in October.

In addition to these major atrocities, there were many cases involving smaller numbers of killed and disappeared. The Commission details them in a long table under paragraph 886. I went through and recorded every episode that had a definite date. In cases where it said something like 'around 10-12 September,' I allocated them a bit arbitrarily. The results appear in the list below. The process was difficult, and someone else's count might be slightly different, but the patterns are clear enough. The results are:

- 74 incidents occurred in the eight days from 4 September (announcement of the poll results) through 11 September (just before Indonesian President Habibie and kingmaker General Wiranto announced that they would accept peacekeepers).
- The next five days (12-16 September) were a second, less intense phase, with 27 incidents.
- The following four days (17-20 September) saw five incidents.

Put another way, the first period saw an average of 9.25 incidents per day, the second saw 4.5, and the last period saw 1.25.

So it seems clear that the violence was subsiding by the time the Australian troops arrived. Once they had arrived, signalling a humiliation for the Indonesian military, a number of further incidents did accompany the beginning of the Indonesian withdrawal. The Commission records seven incidents on 21 and 22 September and a number thereafter. It attributes some of this to the TNI rather than the militia. On the other hand, John Martinkus reports militia violence after the troops arrived, which he ascribes to them being 'cornered' after they were abandoned by the TNI.[163] Whatever the exact interpretation, this final spasm of violence wasn't prevented – if anything, was caused – by the arrival of the Australians.[164]

Further interventions

Clinton's behaviour shocked some in the Australian foreign policy establishment, while another former diplomat, Duncan Campbell, recalled precedents from the sixties:

> The great Australian expectation of US combat commitment to us everywhere in the Malay world must be permanently purged. The US dumped us over West New Guinea, refused to define ANZUS to include Borneo during Sukarno's confrontation of Malaysia, and insisted the Commonwealth alone made defence arrangements for Malaysia and Singapore.[165]

Against this background, we can better understand John Howard's eagerness to send significant forces to Iraq and Afghanistan. The US indifference to the East Timor crisis suggested that Canberra was not paying enough dues to the US to persuade it to underwrite the Australian sphere of influence in the Asia-Pacific. The next opportunity to do so arrived with the 'War on Terror' after 9/11. The Howard government then allocated $5.6 billion to transform much of the army into state-of-the art expeditionary land forces.[166] Such forces were suited to policing the South Pacific as well as to joining US adventures around the globe. They were not so suited to defending you and me from actual threats; but then, there were no such threats.

Howard's Timor success opened the door for a series of local interventions around the region, beginning with the Solomon Islands. In the Solomons, economic tensions had led to a polarisation between ethnic groups. The Malaita Eagle Force based itself on new settlers, drawn to the capital and its surrounds, who were in conflict with Guadalcanal people. A pattern of warlordism ensued, and Canberra organised the Regional Assistance Mission to Solomon Islands (RAMSI) intervention on both military and civil-society levels to assert Australian control.

Problems arising from neoliberal policies had provided the pretext for direct neo-conservative military and political intervention in the Solomons. The government-funded Australian Strategic Policy Institute (ASPI) had remarked in a report called *Beyond Bali* that, while Australian policy since decolonisation had consistently stressed the need to allow countries to manage their own problems, it now seemed that this approach would no longer work.[167] The subsequent ASPI report, *Our Failing Neighbour*, called the Solomons a failing state requiring a multinational effort at rehabilitation. The authors were jumping aboard the 'War on Terror' bandwagon.[168]

In 2002, the Solomons had asked the IMF, the World Bank and 'donor countries' for an injection of cash. Canberra led the charge to demand, in return, a further slashing of jobs and government spending. At the same time, Honiara ceded control of its finances by appointing New Zealand 'reform' consultant Lloyd Powell to head its finance department. Still, as late as January 2003, Alexander Downer had dismissed calls to send troops as folly. It would be hard to explain to taxpayers, he said; and it would mean an open-ended commitment without an exit strategy. 'Foreigners do not have the answers for the deep-seated problems affecting the Solomon Islands.' After the invasion of Iraq, this tune changed. Suddenly, it was urgent to deal with a failed state which might spawn terrorists, and the people of the Solomons must be protected from violence.[169] The importance of the position of Secretary-General of the Suva-based forum secretariat increased; Australian Greg Urwin took the reins, imposed by Howard over stiff opposition. Previously, the position had always been held by a Pacific Islander.

The imperialist push continued on several fronts. The Australian 'Defence' Force continued to expand its island 'peace keeping' role. Canberra also expanded its humanitarian efforts – most notably in Aceh after the tsunami, where the Australian military competed for kudos with the US marines. Between 1999 and 2007, the Howard government deployed 68,000 ADF personnel in 10 major overseas missions. Meanwhile, just as an easy initial success in East Timor had paved the way for other interventions further east, so a quick initial success in the Solomons created the climate where an internationalisation of the Australian Federal Police (AFP) was publicly acceptable.

This process passed through a number of stages: unarmed police sent to Timor for the 1999 ballot; investigation of the Bali bombings; and RAMSI. It appears that about 30 officers were working in Indonesia in 2013, the same year in which the Australian SAS were supposed to be engaged in joint exercises with their Indonesian equivalents in Kopassus.[170] These efforts have intensified a peculiar Australian tendency to think certain places belong to

Australia when they don't – for example, Bali, Anzac Cove and Kokoda. None of this even touches on the distortions introduced to island societies, such as Nauru, who find themselves reluctantly hosting large refugee camps.[171] Internationalisation of the AFP has run parallel with new quasi-civilian roles for the military. In August 2001, the Norwegian ship *Tampa* rescued 438 Afghans from a fishing vessel. The Afghans wanted passage to Christmas Island, but Howard sent the SAS to seize the boat. In 2004, the government created an AFP International Deployment Group; in 2006, it strengthened this group by about 400 personnel, taking the total to 1,200 – including an Operational Response Group to deal with 'emerging law and order issues'.[172] Commentator Bruce Haigh remarked in *Online Opinion* that, under the 'unchallengeable mantra of terrorism,' AFP chief Mick Keelty was engaged in empire building with minimum accountability.[173] Their role doesn't always seem to withstand scrutiny: the regional police chief says that almost 1,900 Afghans detained by Australian forces in Afghanistan's Oruzgan Province up to 2013 may have been falsely accused.[174]

Another important Australian initiative is the Jakarta Centre for Law Enforcement Cooperation, to which Canberra committed $37 million when it opened in 2004. As of March 2007, it claimed to have trained nearly 1,700 cops from 33 countries. Initially a joint venture with the Indonesians, it now has a range of European supporters plus New Zealand, according to its annual report.[175]

The new state of East Timor had difficulty in fully establishing itself and was facing new unrest by 2006. Australian forces returned to the country to restore order and, in doing so, made Canberra's colonial attitudes evident. As the progressive NGO *L'ao Hamatuk* told an Australian Senate enquiry, the Australian military refused to place its forces under United Nations command. The East Timor Government opposed this position, but to no avail. Britain and the US backed Australia, which had, after all, established an imperial track record.[176]

Canberra was in a weaker position to confront a coup in Fiji. On 5 December 2006, Fiji's armed forces chief Frank Bainimarama sacked Prime Minister Laisenia Qarase, his Cabinet and senior officials – including Police Commissioner Andrew Hughes, an Australian Federal Police officer. This was partly about unresolved conflicts from a previous coup. The Qarase government planned to pardon rebels who had almost killed Bainimarama in the year

2000. That infuriated Bainimarama, and he had supporters. Some business interests were pleased to see the end of Qarase because he proposed to hand ocean foreshores back to villagers, threatening tourist industry profits.

And the Fijian military had another card to play: hostility to Australian and New Zealand domination. Andrew Hughes made a passable hate figure, having pursued investigations against high-profile citizens. Bainimarama's interim Prime Minister, Jona Senilagakali, told the media that Hughes was promoting Australian foreign policy. In fact, events had exposed the many weaknesses of Australia and New Zealand. New Zealand Prime Minister Helen Clark tried to broker a pre-coup settlement but got nowhere. Australia sent three warships to the region, which Defence Minister Brendan Nelson suggested might discourage a coup, but they just gave the local military an excuse for a show of force.

This contrasts with events in neighbouring Tonga, where street protests and riots shook the authoritarian regime of King George Tupou V in mid-November. After non-violent demonstrations and strikes failed to bring about a transition to democracy, crowds burned down 80 per cent of the central business district. This finally seemed to force democratic concessions, but Australian troops from the same three ships promptly landed to shore up the regime.

Howard loved to talk of defending democracy, but his forces protected a hereditary monarch during pro-democracy unrest in Tonga and let democracy go in Fiji. One reason is that Tonga only had a token army, whereas Fiji's troops know to fight, having been blooded as 'peacekeepers' and mercenaries in the Middle East. In general, Howard avoided casualties for political reasons – and also because he actually cared little for democracy; what he wanted was *order* in the region.[177] This helps us understand Canberra's cautious response to the 1997 Sandline mercenary affair.

Unable to defeat insurgents on Bougainville, despite access to helicopters and other material aid from Australia, PNG Prime Minister Julius Chan contracted South African mercenaries to finish the job. But the PNG military asserted its right to a monopoly of armed force in Operation *Rausim Kwik* (Kick'em out fast), and Chan lost government. Although Chan expected Australian backing and received the gift of many bottles of Clare Valley red from Australian Foreign Minister Alexander Downer, Canberra held back. That didn't mean that the Howard government wasn't capable of intervening; in

Townsville, the Third Brigade was readied for instant deployment to Port Moresby. Perhaps force projection capacity would have been strained, but more than that, Australia feared the destabilising impact of direct ADF action.[178]

Selected Australian troops spearheaded the Solomons action, and others were ready for PNG; but more significant in the long term was Australian administrators taking over key posts in the state machine. Howard secured formal endorsement for this from the Pacific Islands Forum, and he made a major effort to get a stranglehold on PNG public administration.

Papua New Guinea is vastly more important for Australian capital, which dominates the country's economy as its largest trade partner and source of foreign investment. PNG is the world's fourth-largest gold producer, and Canberra wants mining companies to have maximum freedom to operate there. In December 2003, the Australian Government used aid to pressure PNG into accepting Australian appointments to senior jobs in its public service, police and courts. Nauru was similarly obliged to accept Australian bosses for its police and finance department. Foreign capitalists and a narrow layer of well-connected politicians and local business types have grown fat in recent years from an enormous resources boom. The costs of this boom have been borne by rural communities whose land has been seized and environment despoiled. Alongside commercial ventures by Australian companies, Australian governments have pursued a neo-colonial political project.

Most dramatic was the 2003 Enhanced Cooperation Program (ECP), an attempt by the Howard government to seize control of the upper levels of the PNG state machinery – courts, police, and the finance, immigration, border security and aviation departments. Threats by Australia to reduce foreign aid forced Port Moresby to concede. The ECP was only wound back when the PNG Supreme Court struck down legal immunity for Australian Federal Police in 2005. Legal immunity, also known as 'extra-territoriality,' is regarded in Asia as an intolerable throwback to colonial rule.

But hadn't these 'failed states' lost control? Hadn't they squandered aid? ASPI claimed that their continued viability was 'now uncertain,' so didn't they need Australians to come in and fix things? While there were, and are, serious problems, we should not generalise. Unlike the Solomons or Fiji, most Polynesian and Micronesian states have not experienced ethnic conflicts. Many of their difficulties, conversely, are those troubling much of the world, including unemployment, sex tourism and HIV and other serious pandemics. Some regimes are repressive and corrupt, but Fiji's 1997 constitution has better human rights provisions than our own. The Bishop of Malaita wrote, during the Solomons intervention: 'the Solomon Islands have serious economic and security problems but they are not in a state of anarchy and chaos.'[179]

But wasn't PNG falling apart when Howard decided to act? AusAID said in 2003 that life expectancy there had risen, infant mortality had declined, and literacy had improved since independence in 1975. Retiring head of the Pacific Islands Forum Noel Levi told Radio Australia in 2003 that lawlessness in Port Moresby was similar to big Australian cities.[180]

'Predatory wars of plunder'

On 2 August 1990, Iraq invaded Kuwait. Four days later, the UN Security Council unanimously approved a trade embargo on Iraq. A blockade followed, as the US assembled a multinational task force of 40,000 troops. 'Observers noted how hastily Prime Minister Bob Hawke met a US request to send Australian ships to the Persian Gulf.'[181] There was considerable public resistance to the war; Hawke adviser Hugh White would later remark with some asperity:

> it is hard now when we seem to send off troops at the drop of a hat to remember what it was like for Australia to be a country that didn't ever use armed force.[182]

Here was the Vietnam Syndrome once again. Anti-war demonstrations began.

The anti-war actions were substantial, but Australia's government was still one of the first to join the coalition force. Bob Hawke was keen to get Australia involved, mainly by contributing warships. Its forces were formally deployed under the auspices of the United Nations; in practice, they served under US command. The war climate boosted the PM's standing at a time when Paul Keating was plotting a leadership challenge. Keating had to wait until the war ended to challenge the man he took to calling 'Napoleon without a hat.'[183] With the ships, Australia managed a somewhat more substantial contribution than in some previous wars. Having learned a bitter lesson about the fragility

84   THE NEIGHBOUR FROM HELL

Australian Defence Force international missions in the Solomon Islands.
Source: Department of Defence

of US public sentiment during the 1999 East Timor crisis, Canberra was inclined to invest more in insurance. It was, however, still modest in scope and primarily symbolic.

There were clear parallels between Bob Hawke and John Howard's handling of the Gulf and Afghan wars, beginning with their enthusiasm. After 9/11, when the shape of the US 'war on terror' was not yet entirely decided, Howard was saying clearly, in public and in private, that troops would probably be needed. When President Bush rang, Howard readily assented. He later described their exchange as having 'freshened up the alliance.'[184] That was an understatement. Bob Woodward related the PM's interaction with President Bush: 'far from being reluctantly dragged into a war, John Howard was among its most energetic promoters...barracking, urging, pledging...'[185] Even the largest global anti-war protests ever seen couldn't prevent an invasion when the politicians were so determined to stage one. On 20 March 2003, a combined force of US, British and Australian troops, under US leadership, invaded Iraq in the Second Gulf War (leaving aside the Iran–Iraq conflict). They claimed to be looking for weapons of mass destruction. They found nothing of the sort, but they did unleash years of bloodshed across Iraq.

TESTING THE VIETNAM SYNDROME   85

Small but effective Australian detachments assisted, notably the SAS, which came out of the shadows to a degree. Australian participation gained the government considerably better access to intelligence, including the presumption of automatic release of sensitive information. And the price wasn't high: Australian units just had to be there and lend their name. This was because so few countries were prepared to sign up for the 'coalition of the willing' which fought the war. The United Nations was sidelined, and the major European powers were hostile to this demonstration of power by the English-speaking countries and their neo-conservative ideologues.

In his 2005 Menzies Lecture, Australian ambassador to the US Michael Thawley declared that, whatever you thought of Howard's decision to join the war in Iraq, it was taken independently. This was broadly true. Tony Kevin, a critic, says that after 9/11, Howard's approach to the Bush agenda was 'to hype it up' from the beginning. Lloyd Cox and Brendon O'Connor cite Thawley, and they add:

> Far from being coerced into the war by an overbearing US administration...the Australian government manifested an uncommon enthusiasm for war. Its energetic support of the US in the United Nations, its many hawkish public statements on the need to confront Iraq, and its pre-deployment of armed forces to the Persian Gulf despite the absence of any formal request from Washington, all bespoke a resolute commitment to militarily support a US invasion...Indeed, it was not implausible to suggest, as critics did, that the Australian government 'seemed even more determined than the United States in their intent to confront Saddam Hussein over his alleged possession of weapons of mass destruction.'[186]

The Labor Party had opposed the 2003 Iraq war and, having won government in 2007, ended commitments in Iraq. But it plodded on in Afghanistan, with Julia Gillard and Tony Abbott a familiar duo at military funerals. The Coalition, mildly embarrassed by what was seen as a premature decision to pull out of Afghanistan early in the decade, sent a new expeditionary force. Essentially, however, the views of the two sides of parliament were very close.[187] In the background, the West tried unsuccessfully to get a grip on Afghanistan.

Australia was the first nation to commit itself, to the point where Richard Ackland observed: 'you would think this is mainly Australia's war.'[188]

Efforts are made to show us portrayals of diggers operating at a morally high level. Yet, all too soon, we hear of their sins of omission, as when they handed over prisoners for interrogation at the merciless hands of the pro-government Afghan army. When the latter turned up, according to a military source, captives got the 'look of death' in their eyes. 'They were shitting themselves,' says the source. At the other end of the scale was the bizarre 'Weekend at Bernie's' incident, where a dead Taliban arrived at the Australian base, then departed in a taxi while Australian officers fought over who was responsible for the remains.[189]

For those who might see the Afghan intervention as pursuing humanitarian goals, *The Age* reported in 2013 that military spending for Afghanistan had outweighed development aid by about seven to one. It pointed out that Australia is withdrawing aid along with the troops:

> The overall aid budget will fall to 0.33 per cent of gross domestic product and the defence budget will rise to 2 per cent, in an increase 10 times as big as the aid cut.[190]

Public support for the Afghan adventure began to drop from 2008, with polling consistently showing majorities for ending the war. It retained bipartisan parliamentary support, which enabled the Rudd–Gillard government to stay the course, even though the ADF was taking casualties. The government tried to sustain support by invoking Anzac and glorifying the SAS (who apparently did most of the fighting);[191] but publicising SAS casualties had a political cost, even though the ADF is much more restrictive towards the media than the US military.[192] When the exercise finally ended, both sides of politics breathed a sigh of relief. The Vietnam Syndrome had been beaten, but only in a superficial sense.

An element of continuity for the US alliance is provided by the US communication bases. It is now more than three decades since Des Ball published his critique about the US bases in Australia, and the People for Nuclear Disarmament movement put the spotlight on these high-tech spooks.[193] Their activities and physical location both evolve, but the relationship between the

US and Australian sides remains fairly constant or, indeed, grows stronger. The US intelligence facility at Pine Gap, near Alice Springs, has greatly expanded its primary signals intelligence function monitoring missile testing and has also expanded its secondary role to include collection of signals intelligence vital for US conventional war activity in the wars in Iraq and Afghanistan and in US-led global counter-terrorism. The bases make an obvious contribution to the US alliance by keeping the US engaged in this part of the world. One US official has said that the US would 'never fight another war in the eastern hemisphere without the direct involvement of [the base at] Pine Gap.'[194]

It can get close and personal. Surveillance of near neighbours is intense.[195] In July 2013, Fairfax reported that Pine Gap had played a key role in the 'targeted killing' of Al-Qaeda and Taliban leaders, as well as the rather less targeted murder of civilians. Many drone strikes use targeted data from Pine Gap. To get a sense of scale, compare this: a leaked Pakistani Government document named 746 people killed by drones between 2006 and late 2009. This included 147 civilians, 94 of them children.[196]

George Orwell is said to have remarked that no situation is so dire that it can't be made worse by the arrival of a policeman. The same applies to imperialist forces. Africans have more to worry about these days, now that a squadron of SAS has been operating at large there, including in Zimbabwe, Nigeria and Kenya. The squadron, based in Queenscliff, Victoria, was raised under Howard but given a new intelligence focus under Kevin Rudd. The intelligence/combat combination mirrors US methods and will allow for increased joint activities.[197] It also keeps the Australian forces close to the US as the US and France help to escalate the plunder of Africa. As I write this in 2014, the United Nations has authorised Western and other forces to invade the Central African Republic, and Australian police have established a presence in South Sudan. Similarly, the emerging China–US tensions offer opportunities to apply the 'insurance policy,' beginning with playing host to the US marines.

Yet another outrage demands our attention. Launching an exercise in political polarisation before the 2007 federal elections, John Howard startled the public by sending the ADF against Indigenous communities in what has become known as the Northern Territory Intervention. This could be understood as an extension of domestic powers to the military, a trend discussed earlier; equally, we could see it as a new imperialist venture. 'Operation Outreach,' the intervention's main logistical operation, was conducted by some 600 soldiers and detachments from the ADF.

Militarist circles have shown a nervous touchiness when these actions are criticised. The Australia Defence Association (ADA) warned against 'scaremongering,' calling the interventions a 'whole of government' effort. But so was the Vietnam War. The ADA cited a 2006 call from a leader of the Australian Medical Association for an ADF 'peacekeeping' force to be deployed in Aboriginal communities. The analogy is indeed apt; such forces are an arm of imperialism.[198]

The intervention aims to shatter the fragile survival frameworks of Indigenous people and to force them into a conventional economic framework. Nicholas Rothwell described it in *The Australian* as a program of neo-assimilation and 'the inglorious close of the era of self-determination.'[199] Much of the theory behind it came from Helen Hughes, an author of some of the recent neoliberal policy for the Pacific islands who was associated with ASPI. Since the 1970s, Hughes argued, Australia had been conducting 'a socialist experiment in remote communities with the lives of Aborigines and Torres Strait Islanders.' A blueprint entitled *A Certain Heritage* was allegedly provided by Coombs, Brandl and Snowdon. It advocated communal land ownership, supported by substantial welfare transfers, to create 'an Aboriginal utopia.'[200] Needless to say, it was, and is, far from a utopia.

Translated into everyday terms, what Hughes called a 'socialist experiment' flowed from a series of victories won by Indigenous people and their supporters in the land rights struggles of the 1960s through 1980s. The out-station culture that resulted represented a last chance for many to create a means of survival for their cultures, and even for themselves. It offered a small space, free of the worst cruelties of white dominated capitalism.

The first chapter of this book noted that the colonisation of this continent and surrounding islands, which began after the first fleet's arrival in 1788, failed to convince or intimidate Indigenous people into embracing a system of profit making and wage labour. Hughes' words echo those of the 19th century clergyman quoted earlier. Aboriginal 'socialism' – a collectivist ethos in the Indigenous cultures – can indeed clash with capitalism, by its nature. The state and capital could tolerate this if it was just another policy issue. It became intolerable when the legislation and court decisions granted rights to Aboriginal and Torres Strait Islander people. That created a legal requirement for representatives of capital to negotiate with Indigenous people almost – for a fleeting moment – as equals. Then the gloves came off; the pretences were discarded; the politics of imperialism returned.

And with it, the need for a new politics of resistance.

Further reading

Tom Bramble, 'Australian Imperialism and the Rise of China', *Marxist Left Review*, no. 3, Spring 2011.

Alex Callinicos, *Imperialism and Global Political Economy*, London, Polity Press, 2009. The author's methodology may be controversial, but the book is rigorous and comprehensive.

Lloyd Cox and Brendan O'Connor, 'Australia, the US, and the Vietnam and Iraq Wars: Hound Dog, Not Lap Dog', *Australian Journal of Political Science*, vol. 47, no. 2, June 2012.

Diane Fieldes, 'The NT Intervention: The Liberal Defence of Racism', *Marxist Left Review*, no. 1, Spring 2010.

Cameron Forbes, *The Korean War: Australia in the Giants' Playground*, Melbourne, Pan MacMillan, 2010.

Kevin Foster, *Don't mention the war: The Australian Defence Force, the media and the Afghan conflict*, Clayton, Victoria, Monash University Publishing, 2013.

Michael Kidron, "Imperialism", in his *Capitalism and Theory*, London, Pluto, 1974. An iconoclastic critique.

Humphrey McQueen, *A New Britannia*, Melbourne, Penguin, 1978.

John Newsinger, *The Blood Never Dried: A People's History of the British Empire*, London, Bookmarks, 2010.

Tom O'Lincoln, *Australia's Pacific War: Challenging a National Myth*, Melbourne, Interventions, 2011.

Gregory Pemberton, *All the Way: Australia's Road to Vietnam*, Sydney, Allen & Unwin, 1987.

Henry Reynolds, *The Other Side of the Frontier*, UNSW Press, 1981. Part of an important discussion on Aboriginal resistance.

Wayne Reynolds, *Australia's Bid for the Atomic Bomb*, Melbourne University Press, 2000.

Derrick Scarr, *The History of the Pacific Islands: Kingdoms of the Reefs*, Melbourne, MacMillan, 1990.

Roger Thomson, *Australian Imperialism in the Pacific: The Expansionist Era*, Melbourne University Press, 1980.

Endnotes

AUTHOR'S ORIGINAL INTRODUCTION

1   Quoted in B. Wurth, *1942: Australia's Greatest Peril*, Macmillan, Sydney, 2008, p. 145.

2   A. Broinowski, *Howard's War*, Melbourne, Scribe, 2003, pp. 3, 17.

3   R. Evans, 'Forgotten War', *The Age*, 10 August 2013, p. 24. Evans' description of how Reynolds sees colonial Australia.

4   Quoted in introduction to J. Doyle, J. Grey and P. Pierce, *Australia's Vietnam War*, Texas A&M University Press, 2002.

5   Quoted in Doyle, Grey and Pierce, *Australia's Vietnam War*, p. 7.

6   C. Stewart, 'Spies Like Us', *Weekend Australian Magazine*, 10-11 November 2001.

7   Karl Liebknecht, 'The Main Enemy Is in Your Own Country!' *Socialist Appeal*, vol. III, no. 21, 4 April 1939, p. 3.

8   V. Lenin, 'Imperialism', in *Selected works [of] V. I. Lenin*; One-volume edition, New York, New World paperbacks, 1971.

9   Lenin, 'Imperialism', p. 171.

10 See M. Kidron, 'Imperialism' in his *Capitalism and Theory*, London, Pluto, 1974; and T. Bramble, 'Is There a Labour Aristocracy in Australia?' *Marxist Left Review* no. 4, Winter 2012. Speaking at the Fifth Asian Global Justice School, 5 July 2013 in Manila, I rashly offered a new argument: that Lenin had sought to theorise imperialism and resistance in two ways, mostly overlapping but not always compatible. One was to make a case for the strategic necessity of allying oppressed nations with the Communist International; the other was to analyse the development of the 'highest stage of capitalism.' In the second endeavour, which was really a research program in its own right, he got a bit lost. It was the first that really mattered. (See photo from this talk on back cover)

11 Lenin, 'Imperialism', pp. 179-180.

12 R. Maddock and I. McLean (eds.), *The Australian Economy in the Long Run*, Melbourne, Cambridge University Press, 1987, p. 11.

13 Lenin, 'The Report of the Commission on the National and Colonial Questions', http://rawlinsview.com/201e/11/04v-i-lenin-preliminary-draft-of-these-on-the-national-and-colonial-questions/. There are similar statements in 'Imperialism' and elsewhere.

14 K. Marx, *Capital*, various editions, part viii.

15 E. Emmanuel, 'White Settler Colonialism and the Myth of Investment Imperialism', *New Left Review*, no. 73, May–June 1972, p. 39.

16 The academic Stewart Firth has remarked: 'the existing model is really very much a securitised model…it's about regional security and Australian security. We're intervening in this region, and we're attempting to improve governance outcomes and so on… So the model is really built around a security approach.' Correspondents Report, 'The Pacific "arc of instability"', ABC Radio, 20 August 2006.

17 Lansdowne quoted in M. Dunn, *Australia and the Empire*, Melbourne, HarperCollins, 1984, p. 8.

INTRODUCTION TO THE SECOND EDITION

18 Ill health prevented Tom O'Lincoln from writing this new introduction himself. He confirmed his agreement with the general analysis presented here, but responsibility is the author's alone.

19 Measured by gross domestic product (GDP) in constant US dollars. Author's calculations from World Bank data, as at September 2020.

20 Measured in constant US dollars. Author's calculations from Stockholm International Peace Research Institute *SIPRI Military Expenditure Database*, as at September 2020.

21 Department of Foreign Affairs and Trade, 2020 *Composition of Trade Australia 2018–19*, Table 9.

22 For a detailed assessment from a Marxist perspective, see T. Bramble, 'Australian imperialism and the rise of China', *Marxist Left Review*, no. 3, Spring 2011.

23 Department of Defence, *2013 Defence White Paper*, 2013, p. 11.

24 Department of Defence, *2020 Defence Strategic Update*, 2020, p. 11.

25 Scott Morrison, *Address to the Aspen Security Forum*, 5 August 2020.

26 S. Dziedzic and A. Greene, 'US official urges Australia to participate in South China Sea freedom of navigation operations', *ABC News*, 27 July 2020.

27 Department of Defence, *Pacific Maritime Security Program*, www.defence.gov.au/annualreports/17-18/Features/Maritime.asp.

28 D. Wroe, 'Australian Navy to use overhauled PNG military base as China concerns grow', *The Sydney Morning Herald*, 1 November 2018.

29 M. Doran and S. Dziedic, 'Deal to be inked for Solomon Islands undersea internet cable Australia stopped China building', *ABC News*, 13 June 2018; P. Begley, 'Sea cable boosts ties to PNG, Solomon Islands amid China influence', *The Sydney Morning Herald*, 28 August 2019.

30 Department of Foreign Affairs and Trade, *Papua New Guinea Development Cooperation Fact Sheet* February 2020.

31 M. Clarke, 'Australia's $440m loan to PNG "completely unrelated" to countering China, Finance Minister says', *ABC News*, 25 November 2019.

32 *Forum Communiqué, Fiftieth Pacific Islands Forum*, 13–16 August 2019, p. 4.

33 K. Lyons, 'Revealed: "fierce" Pacific forum meeting almost collapsed over climate crisis', *The Guardian*, 16 August 2019.

34 B. Smee, 'Pacific islands will survive climate crisis because they "pick our fruit", Australia's deputy PM says', *The Guardian*, 16 August 2019.

35 For an overview of recent debates around the Marxist theory of imperialism and its ongoing relevance, see A. Callinicos, *Imperialism and Global Political Economy*, Cambridge, Polity, 2009.

36 T. O'Lincoln, *Australia's Pacific War: Challenging a National Myth*, Melbourne, Interventions, 2011.

THE NEIGHBOUR FROM HELL

37 Richard Cobden and John Bright were English Radicals and Liberal MPs and strong promoters of free trade policies. Goldwin Smith, also a Liberal, was identified as an anti-imperialist.

38 H. Belloc, *The Modern Traveler*, London, E. Arnold, 1898, n.p.

39 M. Anderson, *The Ascendancy of Europe*, London, Longman, 1972, p. 205.

40 D. Scarr, *The History of the Pacific Islands*, Melbourne, MacMillan, 1990, p. 234.

41 Quoted in H. Reynolds, *The Other Side of the Frontier*, Townsville, James Cook University of North Queensland, 1981, p. 119. For a discussion, see T. O'Lincoln, *United We Stand*, Melbourne, Red Rag Press, 2005, pp. 89–94.

42 *The Australian*, 8 November 1826.

43 E. Tapp, *Early New Zealand*, Melbourne University Press, 1958, p. 8.

44 J. Eddy, *Britain and the Australian Colonies 1818–1831*, Oxford, Clarendon Press, 1969, p. 251.

45 *The Age*, 14 August 1869.

46 Scarr, *History of the Pacific Islands*, p. 188.

47 Scarr, *History of the Pacific Islands*, p. 176.

48 W. Minn, *Nationalism and Federalism in Australia*, Melbourne, Oxford University Press, 1994.

49 John Locke's *Second Treatise of Government*, 1690, offers justifications for colonisation and appropriation of land.

50 *The Age*, 29 May 1883.

51   R. Thomson, *Australian Imperialism in the Pacific*, Melbourne University Press, 1980, p. 64.

52   Thomson, *Australian Imperialism in the Pacific*, p. 69.

53   G. Serle, 'The Victorian Government's Campaign for Federation 1883-1889', in A. Martin (ed.), *Essays in Australian Federation*, Melbourne University Press, 1976, p. 4.

54   Thomson, *Australian Imperialism in the Pacific*, p. 129.

55   G. Serle, *The Rush to be Rich*, Melbourne University Press, 1974, p. 196.

56   Quoted in M. Lake and H. Reynolds, *What's Wrong with Anzac?* UNSW Press, p. 45.

57   S. Alomes, 'Australian Nationalism in the Eras of Imperialism and "Internationalism"', in J. Arnold, P. Spearitt and D. Walker (eds.), *Out of Empire: The British Dominion of Australia*, Melbourne, Mandarin, 1993, p. 174.

58   L. Trainor, *British Imperialism and Australian Nationalism*, Melbourne, Cambridge University Press, 1994, p. 27.

59   Serle, *The Rush to be Rich*, pp. 198, 200.

60   Thomson, *Australian Imperialism in the Pacific*, pp. 103ff, discusses the subtle ways that colonial politicians used the Sudan adventure to strengthen their position.

61   J. Rickard, 'Loyalties', in Arnold, Spearitt and Walker, *Out of Empire*, p. 35.

62   B. Penny, 'The Australian Debate on the Boer War', *Historical Studies*, vol. 14, no. 56, April 1971, p. 544.

63   Eddy, *Britain and the Australian Colonies*, p. 247.

64   S. Ward, 'Security', in D. Schreuder and S. Ward (eds.), *Australia's Empire*, Oxford University Press, 2008, p. 237.

65   B. Nicholls, *The Colonial Volunteers*, Sydney, Unwin Hyman, 1988, p. 136.

66   H. McQueen, *A New Britannia*, Melbourne, University of Queensland Press, 1978, p. 64.

67   Trainor, *British Imperialism*, p. 24.

68   K. Buckley and T. Wheelwright, *No Paradise for Workers*, Melbourne, Oxford University Press, 1988 p. 101-104.

69   Quoted in H. McQueen, *A New Britannia*, p. 10.

70   V. Palmer, *The Legend of the Nineties*, Melbourne University Press, 1988, pp. 67, 72.

71   Quoted in McQueen, *A New Britannia*, p. 31.

72   Penny, 'The Australian Debate on the Boer War', p. 541.

73   McQueen, *A New Britannia*, p. 111.

74   On racism in the context of Australian imperialism, see T. O'Lincoln, *Australia's Pacific War*, ch 4.

75   C. Knapman, 'Reproducing Empire', in S. Magarey, S. Rowley and S. Sheridan (eds.), *Debutante Nation*, Sydney, Allen & Unwin, 1993, pp. 127-8.

ENDNOTES   97

76   T. O'Lincoln, *Australia's Pacific War: Challenging a National Myth*, Melbourne, Interventions, 2011.

77   D. Horner, 'Strategic Policy-Making, 1943–45', in M. McKernan and M. Browne (eds.), *Australia: Two Centuries of War and Peace*, Canberra, Unwin Hyman, 1988, p. 293.

78   A. Callinicos, *Imperialism and Global Political Economy*, London, Polity Press, 2009, p. 165 ff.; K. Nkrumah, *Neo-Colonialism, the Last Stage of Imperialism*, London, Thomas Nelson & Sons, 1966. Available at http://www.marxists.org/subject/africa/nkrumah/neo-colonialism.

79   Quoted in W. Borden, *The Pacific Alliance*, Madison, University of Wisconsin Press, 1984, p. 240 fn 29.

80   Technically, the country was known at the time as Netherlands East Indies; however, Indonesia is used throughout for the sake of consistency.

81   Quoted in Thomson, *Australian Imperialism in the Pacific*, p. 161.

82   Quoted in Thomson, *Australian Imperialism in the Pacific*, p. 215.

83   C. Rowley, *The Australians in German New Guinea 1914–1921*, Melbourne University Press, 1958.

84   Scarr, *History of the Pacific Islands*, pp. 270–71

85   Scarr, *History of the Pacific Islands*, pp. 270–71.

86   D. Denoon, *Getting Under the Skin*, Melbourne University Press, 2000, pp. 17, 23, 40.

87   W. Reynolds, 'Imperial Defence After 1945', in D. Lowe (ed.), *Australia and the End of Empires*, Geelong, Deakin University Press, 1996, p. 128.

88   'Situation of Australian colonies as at January 1944', National Archives of Australia: CP637/1, item 45.

89   'Timor – The Balibo Five', UNSW Canberra, School of Humanities and Social Sciences, online article (no author) https://www.unsw.adfa.edu.au/school-of-humanities-and-social-sciences/east-timor/english/historical-context/independence#:~:text=The%20WWF%20began%20by%20refusing,to%20supply%20the%20Dutch%20effort (accessed 27 September 2020).

90   P. Dorling (ed.), *Diplomasi: Australia & Indonesia's Independence*, Canberra, Australian Government Publishing Service, 1994, pp. 142, 150, 162, 191.

91   M. George, *Australia and the Indonesian Revolution*, Melbourne University Press, 1980, incl. quotes pp. 16–18.

92   D. Jordan, *Conflict in the Unions*, Resistance Books, Sydney 2013, ch 7.

93   D. Black (ed.), *In his Own Words: John Curtin's Speeches and Writings*, Curtin University, Perth, Paradigm Books, 1995, p. 195.

94   W. Reynolds, *Australia's Bid for the Atomic Bomb*, Melbourne University Press, 2000, p. 25.

95   J. Richelson and D. Ball, *The Ties that Bind*, Sydney, Allen & Unwin, 1985.

96 W. Reynolds, *Australia's Bid for the Atomic Bomb*. See also A. Cawte, *Atomic Australia 1944–1990*, Sydney, NSW Press, 1992, pp.106–107, 127; 'Secret Nuclear Testing at Woomera', ABC radio *AM* archives, 2 April 2002, http://www.abc.net.au/am/stories/s518339.htm

97 Quoted in P. Ham, *Vietnam: The Australian War*, Sydney, HarperCollins, 2007, p. 303.

98 Percy Spender and Richard Casey were both foreign ministers in the early 1950s.

99 G. Pemberton, *All the Way: Australia's Road to Vietnam*, Sydney, Allen & Unwin, 1987, pp. 24, 31.

100 Doyle, Grey and Pierce, *Australia's Vietnam War*, p. 9.

101 R. Casey, *Australian Foreign Minister*, London, Collins, 1972, pp. 125, 151–3.

102 P. Kelly, 'No Lapdog, This Partner Has Clout', *The Australian*, 28 August 2002, p. 13.

103 S. Frühling (ed.), *A History of Australian Strategic Policy Since 1945*, Canberra, Defence Publishing Service, 2009, pp. 75, 133–35, 185. This is a collection of documents. Menzies on wooden guns: 'Australia's Forces to Serve Anywhere', *The West Australian*, 23 September 1950, p. 1.

104 D. Dutton, 'An Alternative Course in Australian Foreign Policy', *Australian Journal of Politics and History*, vol. 43, no. 2, April 1997.

105 This comes through in W. McMahon Ball, *Japan: Enemy or Ally?* Melbourne, Cassell, 1948.

106 Dutton, 'An Alternative Course'.

107 R. Trembath, *A Different Sort of War*, Melbourne, Australian Scholarly Publishing, 2005, pp. 53ff.

108 Dutton, 'An Alternative Course'.

109 Quoted in R. O'Neil, *Australia in the Korean War 1950–1953*, Vol 1, Canberra, Australian Government Publishing Service, 1981, p. 65.

110 P. Spender, *Exercises in Diplomacy*, Sydney University Press, 1969, p. 48.

111 J. Hooker, *Korea: The Forgotten War*, Sydney, Time-Life Books Australia, 1989, p. 18.

112 B. Cumings, 'American Airpower and Nuclear Strategies', in M. Seldon and A. So (eds.), *War and State Terrorism*, Oxford, Rowman & Littlefield, 2004, pp. 74–75.

113 S. Lone and G. McCormack, *Korea Since 1850*, Diane Publishing, 1993. There is a plausible case that the US used biological warfare: see S. Endicott and E. Hagerman, *The United States and Biological Warfare*, Indiana University Press, 1998.

114 See C. Forbes, *The Korean War*, Macmillan, 2010, p. 173; R. Perry, 'Australian and British Soldiers Have Been Accused...' *The Times*, 17 June 2011. The northern authorities were accused of 'brainwashing', but, while both political agitation and abuse were used to influence captives politically, the more sinister accusations appear to be baseless; see G. Keckeisen, 'The Korean War "Brainwashing" Myth...' *Military History*, vol. 19, no. 3, August 2002.

115 Willoughby was an admirer of Franco and Mussolini. See Forbes, *The Korean War*, p. 194.

116 Quote in J. Newsinger, *The Blood Never Dried*, London, Bookmarks, 2010, p. 206.

117 C. Bayly and T. Harper, *Forgotten Wars*, Cambridge, MA, Penguin, 2008, p. 419.

118 J. Kent, 'Past lessons for occupying forces', BBC online, 17 July 2004, http://news.bbc.co.uk/2/hi/programmes/from_our_own_correspondent/3897147.stm (accessed 20 September 2020); 'Malayan "Massacre'" Families Seek UK Inquiry', BBC News, 7 May 2012, www.bbc.co.uk/news/uk-17980481 (accessed 30 September 2020).

119 K. Harrison, *Road to Hiroshima*, Adelaide, Rigby, 1983, p. 277.

120 P. Dennis and J. Grey, *Emergency and Confrontation: Australian Military Operations in Malaya and Borneo 1950–1966*, Sydney, Allen & Unwin, 1996, p. 185.

121 R. Komer quoted in Pemberton, *All the Way*, p. 86.

122 A. Balmain, 'Australia's Role in Irian Jaya Takeover Exposed', *The Age*, 26 August 1999, p. 14; H. Lunn, 'How the West Was Lost', *Weekend Australian*, 21–22 August 1999, p. 29.

123 Department of External Affairs, *Current Notes on International Affairs*, Canberra, October 1963, p. 18.

124 J. Mackie, *Konfrontasi*, Melbourne, Oxford University Press, 1974.

125 Quoted in Pemberton, *All the Way*, p 181.

126 *Cited in R. Walsh and G. Munster, Secrets of State, Sydney, Walsh & Munster, p. 3.*

127 Frühling (ed.), *A History of Australian Strategic Policy*, pp. 75, 133–35, 185.

128 J. Roosa and J. Nevins, 'The Mass Killings in Indonesia after 40 years', *Dissident Voice*, 31 Oct 2006, http://www.dissidentvoice.org/Oct05/Roosa-Nevins1031.htm (accessed 30 September 2020); P. Scott, 'The United States and the Overthrow of Sukarno, 1965–1967', originally in *Pacific Affairs*, no. 58, Summer 1985.

129 Quoted in A. Siahaan, 'Historian Claims West Backed Post-Coup Mass Killings in '65', *The Jakarta Globe*, 17 June 2009. http://www.thejakartaglobe.com/news/historian-claims-west-backed-post-coup-mass-killings-in-65/312844

130 K. Kadane, 'Ex-agents say CIA compiled death lists for Indonesians', *San Francisco Examiner*, 20 May 1990.

131 J. Perlez, 'A Former Indonesian Dissident Makes His Peace With America', *New York Times*, 13 February 2003.

132 Quoted by R. Manne in correspondence with G. Henderson, 'Apologetics and Hypocrisy', *The Monthly*, September 2008. www.themonthly.com.au/exchange-australian-anticommunism-and-indonesian-massacre-1965-6-between-gerard-henderson-and-robert.

133 P. Edwards, *A Nation at War*, Sydney, Allen & Unwin, 1977, p. 63.

134 For this section, see also see L. Cox and B. O'Connor, 'Australia, the US, and the Vietnam and Iraq Wars', *Australian Journal of Political Science*, vol. 47, no. 2.

135 Homer Bigart's joke, quoted in S. Jacobs, *Cold War Mandarin*, Baltimore, Rowman & Littlefield, 2006, p. 129.

136 Quoted in R. Kuhn, 'The Australian Left, Nationalism and the Vietnam War', originally published in *Labour History*, no. 72, May 1997, pp. 163–184, https://sa.org.au/interventions/lvframe.htm (accessed 30 September 2020).

137 P. Howson, *The Howson Diaries*, Viking Penguin, 1984, pp. 223, 141; Wilton quoted in Pemberton, *All the Way*, p. 318.

138 Commonwealth Parliamentary Debates, House of Representatives, 29 April 1965, pp. 1060–1; Howson, *The Howson Diaries*, p. 115; Pemberton, *All the Way*, p. 313.

139 Quoted in P. Ham, *Vietnam*, p. 400. Ham's authority is a CIA source.

140 Pemberton, *All the Way*, p. 261.

141 M. Booker, *The Last Domino*, Sydney, Sun Books, 1978, p. 192.

142 *Commonwealth Parliamentary Debates, House of Representatives*, 29 April 1965, pp. 1060–1; F. Frost, *Australia's War in Vietnam*, Sydney, Allen & Unwin, 1987, p. 20.

143 Quoted in G. Woodard, *Asian Alternatives*, Melbourne University Press, 2004, p. 251.

144 Edwards, *A Nation at War*, p. 35.

145 'Troops Will Need Uncommon Virtue', *Weekend Australian*, 18–19 September 1999. I grew up in the US believing just such claims about the US army.

146 Quoted in Ham, *Vietnam*, p. 323.

147 On armoured vehicles, see M. Benns, 'Phantom Force Secrets', *Sydney Morning Herald*, 12 July 2009.

On helicopter killings, see P. Lloyd, 'Aussies Accused of War Crimes in Vietnam', ABC Radio *AM*, 26 June 2001, http://www.abc.net.au/am/stories/s319013.htm.

On water torture, see T. Mcrae, 'Confession of a Digger', *Fraser Coast Chronicle*, www.frasercoastchronicle.com.au/story/2010/04/17/confession-of-a-digger/. The water torture story is reproduced in F. Walker, *Ghost Platoon*, Sydney, Hachette Australia, 2011.

Waterboarding echoes Guantanamo Bay, but the technique is neither new nor especially American. The first cases I know of occurred in the merciless 1898 US campaign to conquer the Philippines. See R. Prevost, 'Water Cure: US Policy and Practice in the Philippine Insurrection', http://www.vsb.org/docs/sections/military/water.pdf. A POW's water ordeal with Japan's Kempetei secret police is described in E. Lomax, *The Railway Man*, London, Jonathan Cape, 1995, pp. 142–143.

148 B. Gibson interviewed in S. Rintoul, *Ashes of Vietnam*, Melbourne, W. Heinemann Australia, 1987, p. 149; see also Z. Ben-Avi interview, p. 165.

149 Ham, *Vietnam*, p. 254.

150 R. Haupt, 'Australia Fights U.S. Asian Retreats', *Australian Financial Review*, 4 October 1977, p. 1; 'Peacock's Plea for US "Strategic Interest in Australia"', 6 October 1977.

151 P. Dibb, *Review of Australia's Defence Capabilities*, Canberra, 1986; 'The Self-Reliant Defence of Australia', http://press-files.anu.edu.au/downloads/press/p68061/mobile/ch01.html.

152 D. Spratt and N. Maclellan, *Winning the War, Losing the Peace*, Carlton South, Alternate News Service, 1991, p. 28.

153 Medical Association for Prevention of War, *Vision 2030: An alternative approach to Australian Security*, 2010.

154 J. Kerin, 'You Police the Pacific: US', *The Australian*, 5 March 2004, p. 1.

155 D. Greenlees, 'Jakarta Threatens to Expel BHP Man', *The Australian*, 18 August 1998, p. 10.

156 See K. Windschuttle, D.M. Jones and R. Evans (eds.), *The Howard Era*, Sydney, Quadrant, 2009, pp. 319-320.

157 Editorial: 'Spending More Makes Sense', *Australian Financial Review*, 15 September 1999, p. 18.

158 Such claims are untrue. See M. McKenna, 'Howard's Warriors' in R. Gaita (ed.), *Why the War Was Wrong*, Melbourne, Text Publishing, 2003.

159 S. Marris and R. Garran, 'Vietnam Hero Back in Action', *The Age*, 15 September 1999, p. 1.

160 For example, G. Sheridan, 'A General Lesson for Government', *The Australian*, 23 June 2000, p. 13, found Cosgrove's ideas 'indispensable' and a 2000 lecture 'masterful'.

161 J. Dunn, East Timor: *A Rough Passage to Independence*, 3rd edn., Longueville Books, 2004, pp. 355-357.

162 *Chega! The Report of the Commission for Reception, Truth, and Reconciliation Timor-Leste*, 2005, https://www.etan.org/etanpdf/2006/CAVR/Chega!-Report-Executive-Summary.pdf (accessed 9 October 2020).

163 J. Martinkus, *A Dirty Little War*, Random House Australia, 2011, pp. 375-378.

164 For a detailed argument about the 1999 events, see S. Pietsch, 'Australian Imperialism and East Timor', *Marxist Interventions*, vol. 2, 2010, pp. 7-38, https://openresearch-repository.anu.edu.au/bitstream/1885/12680/1/Pietsch%20Australian%20imperialism%202010.pdf.

165 D. Campbell, 'Invisible Friends are no Comfort', *The Australian*, 15 September 1999, p. 13.

166 M. Evans, 'Defending the "Special Intersection"', in Windschuttle, Jones and Evans (eds.), *The Howard Era*, pp. 278-306, see p. 292.

167 Australian Strategic Policy Institute, *Beyond Bali*, Canberra, 2002.

168 Australian Strategic Policy Institute, *Our Failing Neighbour*, Canberra, 2003.

169 N. Maclellan, Australia in Solomon Islands, Melbourne, *Nautilus Institute*, 2009.

170 D. Wroe, 'Spying Row with Jakarta May Weaken Australia's Defence', *The Age*, 22 November 2014.

171 See N. Maclellan, 'What has Australia Done to Nauru?' *Overland*, no. 212, Spring 2013.

172 Statement of Prime Minister, 2 February 2004, https://pmtranscripts.pmc.gov.au/release/transcript-21087; PM Media Release 'A Stronger AFP: Responding to Regional Challenges', 25 August 2006, https://pmtranscripts.pmc.gov.au/release/transcript-22436.

173 B. Haigh, 'The Paramilitary Wing of the AFP', *Online Opinion*, 25 February 2008.

174 P. McGeough, 'Many Afghans Held by ADF are Falsely Accused', *The Sunday Age*, 17 March 2013, p. 5.

175 Jakarta Center for Law Enforcement Cooperation, Annual Report, 2012; M. Mellish, 'All quiet for now on South-East Asia Front', *The Australian Financial Review*, 7 March 2007, p. 14.

176 N. Maclellan, *Australia in Timor-Leste: Briefing Book*, Nautilus Institute, 2009.

177 I discuss the Fiji coup in T. O'Lincoln, 'Fiji's New Rulers – Armed and Dangerous', *MR Online*, December 2006.

178 M-L. O'Callaghan, *Enemies Within*, Sydney, Doubleday, 1999; B. Breen, *Struggling for Self-Reliance*, Australian National University Press, 2008, assesses the ADF's capability for Force Projection during the Sandline affair.

179 T. Brown, 'Building a New Strategy for the Solomons', *Australian Financial Review*, 18 July 2003, p. 4.

180 ABC Radio News, 23 September 2003.

181 S. Anson, *Hawke*, Penguin Books Australia, 1991, p. 72.

182 Quoted in B. D'Alpuget, *Hawke the Prime Minister*, Melbourne University Press, 2010, p. 297.

183 P. Kelly, *The End of Certainty*, Allen and Unwin, Sydney, 2008, pp. 625-627.

184 Windschuttle, Jones and Evans (eds.), *The Howard Era*, pp. 325-6.

185 P. Adams, 'Fatal Flaw in Fiasco of a War', *The Australian*, 2 May 2006.

186 L. Cox and B. O'Connor, 'Australia, the US, and the Vietnam and Iraq Wars', *Australian Journal of Political Science*, vol. 47, no. 2, 2012, p. 180; the internal quote is from M. Gurry, 'Issues in Australian Foreign Policy, July to December 2002', *Australian Journal of Politics and History*, vol. 49, no. 2, 2002, pp. 227-43. Specifically, the quotation is on page 228.

187 Two matching anecdotes show the common ground between Labor and Liberal. Paul Strangio relates that, on Whitlam's rise to power, the security agencies were nervous about Jim Cairns being briefed about the communication bases; but Whitlam reassured them that Cairns would never request a briefing. Peter FitzSimons reports that, when the Hawke Government came to power, Kim Beazley was likewise startled to find that Fraser's ministers and officials had much knowledge in their heads

but nothing documented, as if they 'didn't want to know.' This could be a pattern of acquiescence, but it is more likely that such arrangements are designed to give Australian politicians 'deniability' in case of a mishap at one of the facilities. P. Strangio, *Keeper of the Faith*, Melbourne University Press, 2002, p. 287; P. FitzSimons, Beazley, HarperCollins, Sydney, 1998, p. 240.

188   R. Ackland, 'Oh What a Lovely Distraction', *Sydney Morning Herald*, 19 November 2001.

189   D. Rowe and D. Snow, 'Afghans Captive to Murky ADF Protocols', *The Saturday Age*, 18 May 2013, p 18.

190   J. Watson, 'The Lucky Country?' *The Age*, 4 November 2013, p. 18.

191   See B. Nicholson, 'SAS wins with hearts and minds', *The Australian*, 21 July 2012.

192   K. Foster, 'No News is Bad News', in K. Foster (ed.), *What are we Doing in Afghanistan?* Melbourne, Australian Scholarly Publishing, 2009.

193   D. Ball, *A Suitable Piece of Real Estate*, Sydney, Hale & Iremonger, 1980.

194   P. Dorling, 'Pine Gap Drives US Drone Kills', *The Age*, 21 July 2013, p. 1. It isn't due to faintness of heart that the US has doubts about taking control of Asia. Post Cold War Asia is less stable than Western Europe. There are unresolved hostilities between Korea, Japan, Vietnam and China, with no alliance comparable to NATO. The Asian financial crisis exposed the vulnerabilities of most Asian economic powers. Thanks to Nic Maclellan for this insight.

195   P. Dorling, 'Revealed: How Australia Spies on its Neighbours', *The Age*, 31 October 2013.

196   A. Purcell, 'A Dirty Business', *The Age*, 1 August 2013, p. 18.

197   R. Epstein and D. Welch, 'Secret SAS Squadron Sent to Spy in Africa', *Sydney Morning Herald*, 3 March 2012.

198   Australia Defence Association, *ADF support to the federal government's emergency intervention in NT Aboriginal communities*, 2007.

199   N. Rothwell, 'There's No Turning Back Now', *The Australian*, 28 July 2007.

200   H. Hughes, 'A New Deal for Aborigines and Torres Street Islanders in Remote Communities', *Issue Analysis*, Centre for Independent Studies, 1 March 2005. She refers to H. Coombs, M. Brandl and W. Snowdon, *A certain heritage: programs for and by Aboriginal families in Australia*, Canberra, Centre for Resource and Environmental Studies, Australian National University, 1981.

Tom O'Lincoln legacy project

Tom O'Lincoln was born in California in 1947. He grew up in Walnut Creek, east of San Francisco, and attended the University of California, Berkeley. His experiences as an exchange student at the University of Göttingen in 1967–68 had a major impact on the direction of his life. Tom was radicalised and became an activist and a Marxist. In late 1969, he joined the Berkeley branch of the International Socialists (IS). He came to Australia inn 1971. He became involved in revolutionary politics in this country the following year, a commitment that has lasted to the present day.

Starting with the small grouping, the Marxist Workers Group, which became Socialist Workers Action Group at the end of 1972 and the International Socialist in 1975, Tom was a leader and member of various formations which carried through the IS tradition, finally joining Socialist Alternative in 2003. Tom was an activist in many political movements and an active trade unionist as a teacher and in the public service.

Always a keen traveller, Tom witnessed major struggles in Germany, Portugal and Indonesia; he engaged with socialists and activists in countries as far apart as Nicaragua, Peru, Lebanon, Poland, South Korea and the Philippines. He corresponded with, and met, leading socialists in the UK, the US, Germany and elsewhere. His language skills enhanced this experience – Tom could conduct political discussions in German, Russian, Spanish (with some excursions into Portuguese, French and Croatian) and, later in life, Indonesian.

Tom was a prolific writer. He wrote extensively for left-wing newspapers, magazines and websites, including his own website, which he managed for many years. Tom also translated political material into Indonesian and helped to run an Indonesian language website for 10 years.

Tom's political interests are very wide. Having settled here, he made Australia his focus. He published books on Australian history, Australian imperialism, the Communist Party of Australia, the left and social struggles. He contributed works on many international topics, with Indonesia being a special interest during the 1990s. He also wrote on Marxist theory and economics, Stalinism and other theoretical subjects. A list of all Tom's longer works is included in his anthology of essays, *"The Expropriators are Expropriated"*.

Unfortunately, following a diagnosis Parkinson's disease, Tom found it increasingly difficult to continue the creative process. He published the last two of his books with help from others. Tom now lives in an aged care facility, where he has continued his interest in current events and the development of politics in the world.

Some of Tom's books were published with the help of Vulgar Press. Generally, although various imprimaturs were named, the books were effectively self-published, mostly with funds from the Jeff Goldhar Project, a trust fund that provided funding for socialist books. When Interventions was established in 2015 as an independent, not-for-profit radical publisher, we took over Tom's backlist, and published two further works.

All the books before Interventions took over were published conventionally, with print runs determined by finances at the time. Stocks of some books remain, but several are now out of print. Interventions has initiated a project of publishing new editions of all Tom's major works, with new design and new contextual essays by experts in the relevant fields. Importantly, these titles will be added to our current system of print-on-demand, ensuring that the books will never go out of print and Tom's political contribution will always be accessible.

The present book is the first in this project. New editions of *Years of Rage*, *Rebel Women* and *United We Stand* will be published in 2022. The remaining titles will be re-issued when existing stocks are sold and as resources permit.

Tom has been an activist, a revolutionary socialist and Marxist his whole adult life. In his political memoir, *The Highway is for Gamblers*, he writes:

> I have been a Marxist for half a century. In that time I have participated in and been witness to great struggles and momentous historical events. I've had the privilege of standing

shoulder to shoulder with selfless fighters around the world. Those events and the people involved only confirmed in my mind that human liberation can be won through the mass struggles of the working class.

Tom then asks the question, 'Why be a revolutionary socialist today?'. His answer? 'It's a life worth living'. The content of Tom's books has stood the test of time. His is a literary legacy worth preserving and extending to new audiences.

We at Interventions want to keep this legacy alive. Interventions is a not-for-profit association, with no independent source of funding. For more information about the project or to donate please contact info@interventions.org.au.

Janey Stone

PUBLISHED BY INTERVENTIONS

2016 *'The Expropriators are Expropriated' and other writings on Marxism*
2017 *The Highway is for Gamblers: A Political Memoir*

WORKS BY TOM O'LINCOLN TO BE RE-ISSUED

1985 *Into the Mainstream: The Decline of Australian Communism*
1993 *Years of Rage: Social Conflicts in the Fraser Era*
1998 *Rebel Women in Australian Working Class History (co-edited with Sandra Bloodworth)*
2005 *United We Stand: Class Struggle in Colonial Australia*
2011 *Australia's Pacific War: Challenging a National Myth*
2014 *The Neighbour from Hell: Two Centuries of Australian Imperialism*

"**This thought-provoking book challenges us to re-consider what we assumed we knew about the Pacific war.**"

- Dr Peter Stanley, National Museum of Australia

Australia's Pacific War: Challenging a National Myth
Tom O'Lincoln

War is such a nightmare it's hard to believe any war can retain a positive aura for decades. Yet the vast conflict in the Pacific is a shibboleth for Australian politics to this day. Politicians in particular use its appeal to legitimise modern wars. Tom O'Lincoln's book questions every aspect of this syndrome. He argues that the Pacific War was an imperialist one on both sides, that the west cannot claim the moral high ground, and that wartime Australia was riven with class and other social conflicts. His aim is to challenge an Australian national myth.

The Highway is for Gamblers: A Political Memoir
Tom O'Lincoln, with Janey Stone

Tom O'Lincoln's moving political memoir is a testament to a life worth living, in the ranks of those fighting for human liberation. Tom became politicised in the turbulent 1960s and spent decades writing, organising and travelling in a lifelong effort to renew a creative tradition of Marxism in Australia and abroad.

The German student movement, Berkeley radicalism, the Whitlam sacking, the Portuguese and Nicaraguan Revolutions, the Lebanese civil war, dissidence in the Eastern bloc, labour struggles in South Korea, the fall of Suharto – many such episodes are told as eyewitness accounts, amid Tom's reflections on building the International Socialist tradition in Australia. This account of the hands-on building of the Australian radical left, alongside momentous historical global events, is written with a pen that burns with indignation against oppression. Importantly, this is an insight for the activists of tomorrow who hope to change the world.

www.ingramcontent.com/pod-product-compliance
Lightning Source LLC
Chambersburg PA
CBHW072012290426
44109CB00018B/2220